THE MAKING OF A CYBERTARIAT

THE MAKING OF A CYBERTARIAT

VIRTUAL WORK IN A REAL WORLD

URSULA HUWS

MONTHLY REVIEW PRESS
NEW YORK

THE MERLIN PRESS
LONDON

Library of Congress Cataloging-in-Publication Data

Huws, Ursula
  The making of a cybertariat : virtual work in a real world / Ursula
Huws.—1st ed.
    p. cm.
Includes bibliographical references and index.
  ISBN 1-58367-088-2 (pbk.) — ISBN 1-58367-087-4 (cloth)
  1. Employees—Effect of technological innovations on. 2. Information
society. 3. Quality of work life. I. Title.
  HD6331.H89 2003
  331.25—dc21
                                        2003014704

Monthly Review Press
122 West 27th Street
New York, NY 10001
www.monthlyreview.org

Published simultaneously
in the United Kingdom by:
The Merlin Press Ltd.
P.O. Box 30705
London WC2E 8QD
www.merlinpress.co.uk
ISBN 0 85036 537 6

Printed in Canada

10 9 8 7 6 5 4 3 2 1

TO TANSY

TABLE OF CONTENTS

by Colin Leys

THE MOMENTS WHEN A FRESH IMPULSE IS GIVEN to the social sciences by an original spirit deserve to be celebrated, and making the feminist political economy of Ursula Huws available to a wider public is such a moment.

From the late 1970s to the present, while so much intellectual energy was diverted into "culturalism" and postmodernism, not to mention the arid wastes of "public choice," Huws developed a distinctive analysis of *commodification* that combines cultural, economic, social, and political dimensions in an exceptionally innovative and creative way. Among policy makers and researchers concerned with work and technological change her reputation has long been established. But the potential of her work to revivify feminist political economy generally, and to stimulate new research on working conditions, markets, commodification, consumption, and technological change, has not yet been as widely appreciated as it should be. Why this should be so, especially when her writing is so clear, wide-ranging, and witty, might at first sight seem puzzling. The main reason is that very little of her work has been published in academic journals. Huws began writing as a trade union activist in the publishing industry. Her aim then was to reach her fellow workers, who were mainly women, writing in a way they could readily understand and identify with. But this formulation as a writer makes her later, more theoretical essays distinctively accessible and enjoyable. Here, for example, as an appetizer, is how Huws discusses the way in which, according to the apostles of the "weightless economy," the

value of a product is attributable to its sponsor rather than to the labor of
the people who have made it:

> In 1993 . . . Michael Jordan alone received over $20 million from Nike
> for allowing his name and image . . . to be associated with their
> product—equivalent to more than the total labor cost alone for all the
> 19 million pairs of Nike shoes made in Indonesia. Traditional econom-
> ics allows us to understand the very small portion of the final shoe
> attributable to the labor involved in its manufacture as the super-exploi-
> tation of a vulnerable group of workers; the "new economics" simply
> renders them invisible. Yet it is difficult to see the division of labor in
> the production process as anything intrinsically new; rather it can be
> seen as a continuation of a process that has been evolving for at least the
> past century and a half. Michael Jordan may be earning considerably
> more, but his contribution to the value of the final product is not
> different *in kind* from that of the little girls who posed for the Pears Soap
> advertisement at the turn of the century or the members of the royal
> family who gave their official blessing and the use of their coats of arms
> to pots of marmalade. (Chapter 9: "Material World.")

Huws shows how the root of the problems women confront lies in the
way capitalism constantly commodifies traditional tasks, such as cooking,
first making them into paid-for services and finally replacing paid-for
services with the sale of manufactured objects capable of being mass-produced—while simultaneously transferring the remaining labor (self-service
banking, shopping, etc.) to the consumer, with women bearing most of the
costs at every step, both as workers and as "consumers."

As Huws herself notes, part of what she has done is to extend Harry
Braverman's famous analysis of factory work to the analysis of domestic
labor: the "degradation of work" applies to housework, too. But she always
sees these processes in a wider context. She links the situation of a mother
in Milwaukee or Wolverhampton, with her computerized washing machine
and microwave oven, who finds herself spending *more* hours doing housework than her grandmother did before these marvels were invented, to the
situation of another woman in Malaysia who is being super-exploited to

make the computer chips for that washing machine and microwave. In the same way Huws examines how—thanks to modern communications technology—an overworked and underpaid woman worker in a call center in Newcastle or New Brunswick can be threatened with the loss of her job to an even more underpaid woman in a call center in India.

And these are never casually chosen examples. They are based on Ursula Huws's experience as the director of some of the most extensive and sophisticated surveys of work that anyone has done (a full list may be consulted at www.analytica.org.uk.) It was this empirical familiarity with the actuality and interconnectedness of the fast-evolving new forms of human labor produced by worldwide commodification that also allowed her to puncture, so definitively and early, the myth of the "weightless economy" propagated by the evangelists of the 1990s stock market boom.

Another central theme of Huws's work, closely linked to that of commodification in general, is the application of information and communications technology to the labor processes involved in office work. Since the middle of the twentieth century most office work has been done by women. Consequently its transformation through the application of digitized information technology, and through the ability of new communications technology to permit any "digitizable" work to be outsourced to anywhere in the world, to be done increasingly by machines, has primarily (though by no means exclusively) affected women. They have been the labor force chiefly involved, both in pioneering the new technology and in paying the social costs, followed by a new cycle of the degradation of work, and finally job losses.

These themes do not exhaust the analytic tools Huws deploys, but they provide a framework that allows her to illuminate an unusually wide range of contemporary issues: casualization, outsourcing, runaway corporations, the control of computer-based workers through surveillance software, the development of consumer profiles through the computerized tracking of our purchases, the transfer of "consumption work" to consumers, the ideology of "choice," relationships between men and women, "homeworking," loneliness and isolation, the erosion of public space, the dissolution and re-formation of the working class, the work-leisure boundary. Part of the impact of Huws's work when you meet it for the first time is that it sheds a brilliant new light on so much of our contemporary experience.

One more feature of Huws's work should also be noted here: the prescient nature of her predictions. To give just a couple of examples, before the mid-1980s she correctly forecast, contrary to conventional wisdom, the relatively slow take-up of teleworking, broadband cable, and the transitional nature of the boom in data-entry employment. She also correctly foresaw that the dramatic jump in office work productivity predicted in the late 1970s would ensue only when the necessary interfaces between the different information technologies involved had been created, something that conventional wisdom in the mid-1980s was discounting. Huws gets things right because she understands not just the technology, but also the social forces that are driving technological change.

Huws raises the analysis of capitalism's unremitting drive toward commodification to a new level. Understanding this process, and its profound social consequences, has never been more important, and she is a wonderful guide to it.

ACKNOWLEDGMENTS

IN A COLLECTION OF MATERIAL LIKE THIS ONE spanning nearly a quarter of a century, it is impossible even to begin to acknowledge the many friends, collaborators, and mentors who contributed, directly or indirectly, to its contents. I will content myself here with naming just a few of those whose support has been most important.

First, some of the members of the various women's groups with which I was involved when I wrote the earlier pieces and whose insights flowed together with my own, drop by drop, so that it is impossible to distinguish the separate contributions to the collective confluence which emerged. In Yorkshire in the 1970s, these included the West Yorkshire Women and New Technology Group, especially Jude Stoddart, Julia Dick, Lynette Willoughby, and Liz Lancaster and a more private, nameless group, originally convened by Jenny Taylor, which included at various times Sarah Perrigo, Janet Woolf, Jean Gardiner, Shirley Moreno, Lee Comer, Marsha Rowe, Glen Park, Gillian Lacey, Griselda Pollock, and Sue Wilby. Later in London there were three more or less concurrent groups, the—subsequently more formally constituted—Women Working Worldwide, especially Helen O'Connell and Geraldine Reardon; a group originally consisting mainly of women who did some sort of research relating to employment: Jane Barker, Shelley Adams, Ruth Elliot, Mandy Clark, Jane Foot, and Lucy de Groot; and another consisting mainly of writers: Liz Heron, Marsha Rowe (again!), Alison Fell, Rosie Parker, Alison Mitchell, and Maggie Millman. Shirley and

Ruth both died prematurely and are greatly missed; many of he others have remained close and supportive friends. Thank you all.

My second task is to thank Andrew Nash, Michael Yates, and their colleagues at Monthly Review Press for their patience and understanding, and Leo Panitch for introducing me to them. Leo also deserves thanks, along with Colin Leys, his co-editor of *Socialist Register*, for encouraging me to make the time to set down my thoughts. Colin is the most sensitive and modest editor I have ever come across, and I have a great deal to thank him for: the rigor of his (always constructive and gently phrased) criticism as well as his patience and his greatly valued friendship. I am also grateful to Colin, Leo, and their colleague Sam Gindin for convincing me that there is an audience for my ideas. It is to Sheila Rowbotham, however, that I owe the original idea of putting together such a collection of essays. Thank you, Sheila, for your generosity and faith in me over the years.

Finally, I owe a huge debt of gratitude to Peace Rwakeiru who ploughed her way through jumbled mountains of paper to track down the original pieces included in this book, photocopied them, scanned them in for me, carefully checked the scans against the originals and politely but insistently nagged me, over a period of at least two years, to read them through and send them off to be edited. Without her, this book really would not have been published.

INTRODUCTION

THE ARTICLES THAT MAKE UP THE CHAPTERS OF THIS BOOK span a period from the late 1970s to the early 2000s and made their first public appearances in a diverse range of places, some so obscure as hardly to warrant the name "publication." They derive from the interaction between two aspects of my intellectual development: debates carried out in a range of political arenas including the trade union movement, the women's movement, community organizations, and various single-issue campaigns I became involved with over the years; and the evidence collected in the course of my work as a freelancer doing commissioned research, mostly on various aspects of the restructuring of employment and its human impact.

In some ways their production reflects the contradictory forces at play in the life of a freelancer. The self-employed are often envied by those in more traditional employment for our apparent freedom from life in the rut. Instead of an orderly development from one research project to the next, we seem to flit, butterfly-like, from one subject to another. We can follow the scent of an interesting thought trail without bumping up against the barriers of an academic discipline, or the remit of a job description. But the other side of the freelance coin is a state of permanent insecurity. The freedom to take on what work you like is modified by what is available; the freedom to write what you like is modified by what the client will accept; and the freedom for mental exploration is restricted by the time available. When you have enough work, you have no time; when you have time, you have no money.

The essays in this book were not written for money and were thus produced sporadically, in time snatched from other activities. I have sometimes regretted the lack of financial security that prevented me from developing each piece of work to its logical conclusion, yet in retrospect this has its positive side, too. The zigzag progress of my work has enabled me to look at things from a number of different perspectives; to test, so to speak, the view taken from one angle against that from a different approach, at a different time, like a tourist who returns to the same landscape at different times of year, in different company, riding different transport, and using a map of a different scale. Each time only a part of the whole is glimpsed. Yet as the years go by a surprisingly complete and multifaceted picture is built up.

These pieces, then, were informed by the commissioned research I undertook over the years. But they were also informed by my own experiences. The restructuring of employment and of daily life that I was studying in my commissioned work was mirrored in my own experiences and those of my friends and colleagues. Sometimes new research questions were generated, so to speak, from the inside working outward (the process that was called "consciousness-raising" in the early days of the women's movement). At other times the questions came from the outside, from the remits of research clients, the statements of politicians or pundits, or the results of my own research. However, these would then often be tested internally, through examinations of my own experience and discussions with friends.

Perhaps for precisely these reasons the essays in this book are all rooted in a materialist analysis of a kind that started to go out of fashion in the later 1970s but seems to be on the verge of a revival; and underlying most of the essays is a common conceptual framework, or explanatory model.

The model is derived from diverse sources, including Adam Smith, Hegel, and Marx, plus the influence of a free-ranging journey through the radical literature of the 1960s and 1970s, some of which is chronicled in chapter 8 of this volume ("The Fading of the Collective Dream"). That journey is admittedly not extensively documented in the chapters that follow. The freedom to read in libraries and take due note of authors, titles, publishers, places of publication, and page numbers is a luxury for those with salaried academic jobs or ample leisure. Mine was spare-time reading, done on buses and trains, on benches in children's playgrounds, or in bed.

Some of the books were never finished because they were picked up (and faithfully put down again) in friends' houses, or lost, or lent, or because I fell asleep, or the phone rang, or a pressing work deadline intervened, or simply because I found them boring. So while many have left their marks in my thinking, they have not left their references as often or as completely as I would like. And as for the friends who educated me directly, alas, many are no longer alive. Here I remember with particular gratitude and sadness Peter Sedgwick, Henry Neuburger, Jim and Gertie Roche, Don Thompson, Shirley Moreno, Ruth Elliot, and Mike Kidron. I also remember those loved ones who argued so vehemently with my ideas and thereby sharpened them: Colin Richards, Lynette Trotter, Angharad Pimpaneau, and Richard Huws.

So, prefaced with this apology for any omissions in acknowledging the origins of the ideas in these essays, especially to anyone who feels personally unacknowledged, what is the conceptual framework or explanatory model that links the chapters of this book?

Put simply, it is the idea of the commodification process as a central concept in understanding change. By *commodification,* I mean the tendency of capitalist economies to generate new and increasingly standardized products for sale in the market whose sale will generate profits that increase in proportion to the scale of production. In this model, the most obvious example of a commodity is a mass-produced material product, but a commodity may also be a service (for instance a package holiday or an insurance policy), though not all services are (yet) commodities (for example, in most countries primary school education remains uncommodified).

A very schematic historical overview shows a tendency for activities taking place outside the money economy for use or exchange to move into the money economy and be replaced by craft production or consumer services that, generally taking advantage of technological innovations, become the basis of new manufacturing industries which in turn give rise to new service industries (both business-related services and new consumer services). These in turn generate new forms of consumption activities (or, if you prefer, new forms of unpaid labor) that can then form the basis of new consumer service industries and new products, and so the wheel of development keeps turning, generating in the process a multiplication of new commodities and an ever more complex social division of labor.

This model was first put forward in a paper submitted to a working group of the Conference of Socialist Economists in 1979 and is formally published here for the first time, as chapter 1, "New Technology and Domestic Labor." The group's founders had introduced the discussion by arguing that the automation of production would inevitably lead to mass unemployment and a crisis of capitalism because these redundant workers would not have the money to buy the new products that could be produced so efficiently by these now-automated factories.

This "robots don't buy cars" argument (still current two decades later in many circles) puzzled me, because it didn't seem to fit the facts. Looking back over the history of technological innovations it seemed to me that although each wave had undoubtedly led to the pauperization of a large group of workers whose misery should not be discounted, none had led to permanent unemployment across a whole economy. What had happened was that while it had become possible to produce the existing range of products with fewer workers, new commodities had come into existence, forming the basis of new industries that would require a new workforce. The question was, where had these commodities come from? I looked back at previous great waves of innovation. The one that crested in the 1920s and 1930s, powered by electricity, had given us radios, refrigerators, vacuum cleaners, and a range of other domestic appliances. It had mechanized whole areas of domestic life that were previously outside the money economy. Earlier waves had given us factory-made clothes, soap, food, and the like. Could it be that new commodities emerged from the socialization of housework? This was the hypothesis I tentatively explored in the paper. But it did not receive a sympathetic hearing in this male-dominated group, which misconstrued it as a tirade about who should do the housework. After listening to a series of patronizing anecdotal expositions of why washing machines were a good thing, I gave up and withdrew the paper from the book the group was publishing.

Nevertheless, the ideas underlying it continued to ferment and react with others and formed the basis for chapter 2 in this book, "Domestic Technology: Liberator or Enslaver?" Here the context was a women's group, the West Yorkshire Woman and New Technology Group, which had been formed at a socialist feminist conference on women and new technology.

The group was approached by a feminist journal, *Scarlet Woman*, to produce a special issue whose publication coincided more or less precisely with the birth of my daughter. This meant that I could not share in the collective typing, cutting, and pasting which in those days of offset litho printing was the only cheap way to produce the artwork for a journal. But I compensated by writing not one but two articles for it. The first (not included in this collection) drew largely on secondary material to describe the appalling conditions in which young women in developing countries were being obliged to work to produce the silicon chips that formed the building blocks of the new computer hardware. The second (also not included here but subsequently anthologized in a collection of writings from the British Women's Movement) looked at the impact of these technologies on women's unpaid labor.

The analysis of these two essays was taken a little further in an essay written in 1984 and published in 1985 in *Radical Science*. This piece is reproduced here as chapter 3, "Terminal Isolation." I had already written about the home as a site in which production of use values by women's unpaid labor was increasingly being augmented, if not substituted with, the additional unpaid labor of "consumption work." What I wanted to explore was the relationship between this unpaid work in the home and the paid work that was also sometimes carried out there. This was a period when the U.K. government, having privatized British Telecom, was developing strategies to create a communication infrastructure in Britain that would support what were then known as "value-added services." These were supposed to include the potentiality for people to work from their homes and deliver the results through a telephone line. Having recently carried out a survey of people who worked in this way ("the new homeworkers"), I had a lot of raw material on which to draw. I had also recently been rereading Marx and realized that while he wrote a lot about the implications of who owned the means of production, he had not really addressed the question of what one might call the means of *re*production. His analysis of the alienation process assumed that the employer owned the factory and the machines used in production. What happened if the worker worked at home and owned the machines but, unlike the handloom weaver to whom this also applied, was an employee, with work rhythms and targets set entirely by the employer?

Was the trend to owner occupation and the purchase of ever-more expensive and quickly obsolescent technology implicating the working class in its own exploitation to an unprecedented degree? Or was something new going on, which Marx's ideas could not help explain? Chapter 3 attempts to answer this question.

Chapter 4, "The Global Office," dates from the same period but was written for a very different audience. I realized that the same technologies which made it possible for information processing work to be carried out away from the office in someone's home could also be used to relocate it anywhere else in the world where the right infrastructure could be found in combination with a workforce with suitable skills. I started collecting information about this around 1982. "The Global Office" was written to summarize what I had learned so far for a conference designed to encourage fair trading that was organized by the Greater London Council and attended by delegates from developing countries.

Chapter 5, "Challenging Commodification," appeared first in a book edited by a collective of designers. The focus of the book was the idea of workers' alternative plans first promulgated in Britain in the late 1970s by a group of Lucas Aerospace shop stewards and publicized by their charismatic spokesman Mike Cooley. Like many radicals of his generation, Cooley had been recruited by the Greater London Council (in the brief period before it was abolished by the Thatcher government) to help develop worker-centered employment strategies for London. This had brought his work to a wider audience. Although I admired Cooley enormously as an individual, I did not believe that his ideas offered a universal solution. Like many of those promulgated by the Council, they seemed to be rooted in an outdated stereotype of the worker as a wrench-wielding man on a production line, caught, as in a freeze-frame film still, at some moment in the early 1960s when wages were rising, unions were strong, and skills were valued as raw materials, as they were in the slogan with which Harold Wilson won the 1964 U.K. election for the Labor Party—"the white-hot heat of the technological revolution." By then most employment in Britain—and especially in London—was in fact in services, and I wanted to understand why it was so difficult for well-meaning, principled, and altruistic socialist men to come to grips with the idea of service employment as real work. In charting the relationship of this service employment to the rest of the economy, I found myself revisiting the model of commodification I had developed earlier and refining it further, looking in particular at the implications for skills and autonomy both in paid and unpaid work.

Chapter 6, "Women's Health at Work," draws on a different but parallel strand in my life. Since the 1970s I had been involved in various campaigns to improve health and safety at work, especially for women, and I was at the time writing a handbook about office hazards for the London Hazards Centre. A photographic exhibition on women and health was being assembled and I was asked to write an essay about women's health at work for the accompanying catalogue, and this article was the result. The central point is one that emerged again and again from my research: the constituents of well-being at work cannot be understood in isolation. Wherever it is located, and however apparently "mental" the processes involved, the experience of working is one that involves the whole body. How pleasant it is and what actions it consists of result from an interplay between social relations, including the gendered power relations within which it is enacted, and the larger social division of labor.

The subject of chapter 7, "Telework: Projections," is "teleworking," also known as "telecommuting," "networking," "distance work," "electronic homeworking," and a range of other equally inadequate pseudonyms. This essay stands a little apart from the other pieces in this collection, situated closer to my professional "paid for" research and further from my "voluntary" work. The two cannot, of course, be disentangled entirely. I have been involved in a voluntary capacity with a number of campaigns to improve conditions for homeworkers, and of course the commissioned research has also been colored by my own experiences—I have worked from home for most of my adult life. When *Futures* approached me to write this article, I intended it to be my final word on a subject that had become quite boring for me. There seemed, during the 1980s, to be an insatiable interest among policy makers in the subject, and I felt I was being asked endlessly to repeat the answers to the same questions. The concept seemed to me to have become a sort of screen onto which any number of different definitions could be projected and, with them, an equally diverse array of ideological accoutrements. The attempt to nail down the paradigmatic "teleworker" with a fixed definition seemed futile. How wrong I was! The more one denies the existence of a phenomenon the more, it seems, one is seen as an expert on it. Since publishing this piece, I have been unable to escape the subject and doing research on it provides a substantial proportion of my income to this day.

Perhaps it was the end of the Thatcher era, perhaps a change in my personal circumstances (daughter starting secondary school and thus lengthening my working day; taking a job teaching part-time at my local university), but the early 1990s seemed to be a time of taking stock of my intellectual development. Teleworking was not the only subject in which I was becoming aware of a danger of repeating myself. I was also "written out" on the subject of gender and technology, so when I was asked to produce yet another conference paper, I decided to use it as an opportunity to reflect on the development of my thinking on the subject, which was also a history of my interactions with others who were engaging with the same questions, and my reactions to what I had read on the subject. The result is chapter 8, "The Fading of the Collective Dream," which also serves as a commentary on the pieces that precede it.

Then, in the mid-1990s, came the period when the Internet entered daily life. Many of the things I had been writing about in the previous decade became taken for granted, albeit sometimes under different names, and it was no longer necessary to explain the technology before writing about its impacts. This was a prolific period for me in my commissioned work, but I have included no articles from it in this collection until 1999, when, at the height of the dot-com boom, *Socialist Register* encouraged me to write "Material World," which is reproduced here as chapter 9. The friendly reception given to this essay encouraged me to write a second, "The Making of a Cybertariat," chapter 10 in this volume. Each of these pieces has been translated into German and French, and between them they build up a picture of how commodification is reshaping the world in which we now live. "Material World" looks at the ways in which the commodification process has brought new products and industries into being, in new places; the "knowledge" economy is not dissolving the material into thin air but, on the contrary, generating new physical commodities that make voracious demands on the earth's resources. "The Making of a Cybertariat" tracks the new elaborations in the division of labor that accompany these processes and what this means for workers, for their class identities, and for their potential to organize.

The collection ends with "Who's Waiting?: The Contestation of Time," which brings the wheel full circle. Returning to the model of commodification I presented in that first paper in 1979 (chapter 1), this final chapter 11 looks beyond the workplace and back into the home and asks what the impact of these developments is on unpaid consumption work. In particular, it asks whether the Taylorization of service employment—for instance, in call centers—is also leading to a Taylorization of private life, and what this means for human happiness.

The model I have employed has, over the years, helped me come up with counterintuitive answers to a number of questions. Where do new commodities come from? Why doesn't automation lead to mass unemployment? Why is the "knowledge-based" or "weightless" economy associated with growth in the consumption of energy and raw materials? Why don't labor-saving appliances give us more leisure? I hope that the answers proposed in these essays will enable the reader to share some of these insights and in the process give rise to many new questions, as all the best answers do.

/ 1 / NEW TECHNOLOGY AND DOMESTIC LABOR

HARRY BRAVERMAN WRITES in *Labor and Monopoly Capital*:

> As the advances of modern household and service industries lighten the
> family labor, they increase the futility of family life; as they remove the
> burdens of personal relations, they strip away its affections; as they create
> an intricate social life, they rob it of every vestige of community and
> leave in its place the cash nexus.[1]

The history of manufacturing industry over the past 250 years or so can
be seen, very crudely, as the removal, one after another, of tasks performed
for nothing in the home to the marketplace, where they become paid jobs,
performed not for use but for exchange. This process is described as the
socialization of domestic labor. According to Alice Clark,

> In the seventeenth century it [the domestic role] embraced a much
> wider range of production: for brewing, dairy-work, the care of poultry
> and pigs, the production of vegetables and fruit, spinning flax and wool,
> nursing and doctoring, all formed part of domestic industry.[2]

If we look at a broader historical period, and include work normally
done by men, we could extend Clark's list to include production of an even
wider range of commodities: the manufacture of buildings, furniture, shoes,

clothing, agricultural equipment, means of transport, tools, pottery soap, candles, and many others.

The process of socializing the production of these goods had several effects. First, mass-producing the goods in a factory allowed for rationalization of work methods and development of technology which made the goods cheaper, thus making it uneconomic to continue to produce them in the home.

Second, the creative "producing" task disappeared from the home to be replaced by the uncreative task of consuming. Shopping became part of housework, bringing with it dependence on the wage and allowing for the development of the retailing industry.

Third, although many of the jobs created were in fact done by women and children (for example, in the textile industry) the development of manufacturing industry reinforced the divisions between "men's work" (wage-earning work outside the home) and "women's work" (unpaid work in the home) and the introduction of notions such as that of the "family wage."

Side by side with this socialization of manufacturing performed in the home came the socialization of services performed there. Women herbalists and midwives who practiced for nothing on their families and neighbors were replaced by male surgeons and apothecaries who performed for fees and laid the foundations for the modern medical profession and its associated industries. Wise women who arbitrated in disputes were replaced by fee-charging male lawyers. Oral traditions of education were replaced by literary ones—again under the control of men. Complex industries grew up to serve the new needs of exchange and distribution.

This account is, of course, greatly oversimplified. These things did not all happen at once; nor did they happen smoothly. It would be a mistake, too, to believe that the process of socialization of domestic labor is complete; it is still proceeding, and likely to continue to do so. The purpose of outlining its historical development here is to try to begin to unravel the process by which it takes place under capitalism and, more specifically, to look at the part played in this process by the introduction of new technologies. If we can succeed in understanding this process, then it should become possible to predict which new goods and services will come into being as the result of the present spate of investment in microprocessor technology and provide the basis for the next boom. It should also make a contribution toward working out the demands that will achieve a socialization of housework that does not simply trap women (and men) in low-paid, uncreative jobs.

Under capitalism, the purpose of introducing new technology in manu-facturing industry is to produce more goods with less (and preferably cheaper) labor. With each wave of introduction, skilled workers are replaced by machines. And each time there is a large-scale investment in new technology, the same fears are expressed: it will mean massive unemploy-ment and no market for the goods that can be produced by the new methods, because the unemployed workers won't have money to buy them ("robots don't buy cars"). In fact, this has never happened, although there have often been short-term high unemployment and permanent redun-dancy for some individual workers. Each time, as the older industries become more capital-intensive and employ less labor, new industries, usually labor-intensive in their early stages, have come into being, producing new commodities and providing new services.

In the twentieth century, we can see examples of this in the development of industries such as radio, TV, records and hi-fi; frozen foods and other forms of convenience foods; washing machines, refrigerators, and other household appliances; cosmetics; drugs; detergents and other chemicals.

These industries have one thing in common—they all "come from" domestic labor. The commodities they produced have replaced activities carried out in the home by women in the previous generation: singing, reading aloud, playing the piano, and generally providing family entertain-ment, preparing and preserving food, nursing, washing and cleaning.

The generation of women for whom these things were a normal part of housework took for granted things that would have been strange to their grandparents, such as mass-produced shoes and clothing, sewing machines, patent medicines, shop soap, gas, or electric lighting.

One very interesting aspect of this socialization of housework has been that it has not reduced the total amount of time spent on it, as one would logically expect it to. Although new opportunities have been created outside the home for paid labor, the amount of unpaid labor inside the home has remained more or less constant with, if anything, a slight increase.

Ann Oakley collected together the results of the (very sparse) research that had been done on hours of domestic labor, and found that in both rural and urban areas time devoted to housework has not decreased as a result of mass-production household commodities and labor-saving devices. In addition, the quality of the work has not improved either— at least when housework is compared with what are usually seen as the stressful and debilitating types of waged work. The character of housework appears closer to the monotonous, fragmented, and stressful work of unskilled assembly-line workers.[3]

How did this state of affairs come about? Why don't "labor-saving" devices save labor? To begin to get an answer to this question, we need to examine several different factors, some, but not all, directly connected with the way that new technology is introduced. First, the drive for greater routinization of work and increased productivity among service workers has led to an ever-increasing amount of "consumption work" being foisted onto the consumer; for example, collecting your own goods from the shelves of supermarkets and putting your own vegetables into bags; self-service gas stations; automatic cash-dispensing machines in banks, standing in line, so that the time lost is not the waged worker's but the unpaid time of the consumer. Studies of productivity in banks have shown that crucial increases can be achieved by, for instance, getting customers to make out their own deposit slips. Colin Tudge sums up this point nicely:

> The point made about convenience—that a task saved in one place is merely delegated elsewhere—applies equally to economy. The food industry aspires to strip itself of all unprofitable tasks. It does not bring the food to you: you go to the hypermarket. It will only do part of the storage: you need a deep-freeze to cope with its products. Who pays for your petrol? Who for the roads? Who pays for and houses your deep-freeze? All these items, and the time you take traveling to and from the hypermarket, are part of the food bill. They do not appear on the company balance sheets. But they appear on yours, in the end.[4]

Second and similarly, centralization of services transfers expenditure of time, energy, and transportation costs to the user. Examples abound: large supermarkets that serve a wide area, rather than corner shops; having to trail the kids to the outpatients' department of the district hospital, instead of having the doctor come to your house with his little bag of instruments. Again, the incentive to change seems to have come from the need to get greater productivity out of service workers and the proportionally greater investment in technology.

Third, ideological pressures have also played an important part. The development in the early years of this century of the domestic science movement, the germ theory of disease, and the idea of "scientific mother-hood" led to an enormous change in standards of housework: people who had made do with an annual spring cleaning were induced to believe it was immoral to clean less than once a week; people who had been sewn into winter underwear every autumn and unstitched in the spring produced grandchildren who expected clean knickers every day. What began, accord-ing to Ehrenreich and English, as a conscious campaign on the part of the bourgeoisie was taken over by the advertising and public relations industries, which now exhort working-class women to fill their homes with sunlight freshness and comfort softness.[5]

Fourth, one of the consequences of the development of waged work, referred to earlier, was a split between the "public" world of work and the "private" one of the home. The home was expected to provide a haven from the alienated, unpleasant, stressful conditions of the workplace and to provide entertainment, relaxation, emotional support, and sexual stimula-tion and gratification. The burden of satisfying these needs fell to the housewife, although even such needs are becoming socialized. Pleasure, too, has come to be regarded as something that can be bought, leading to the growth of the entertainment industry, amusement arcades, package holi-days, the cosmetics and fashion industries, and pornography. One etymolo-gist has observed that current American usage of language implies that all pleasure is now seen as a commodity that can be acquired and possessed: you "have" fun or sex; or "get" laid or stoned. Compare these with older usages such as "make love" or "make merry."

Despite the fact that fulfillment of these emotional needs has become part of the cash nexus, the responsibility for seeing that they are met is still the housewife's. It is her fault if the home is not happy, and trying to make it so takes up a lot of the time and effort put into domestic labor. These needs are also ones that grow as paid work becomes more boring, repetitive, and stressful—often as a direct consequence of the introduction of new technology.

It is also interesting to look at the time span of the introduction of new commodities and services, which is often rapid. To take one example, the expenditure on radio, electrical, and other consumer durables in the United Kingdom at constant prices (1970 = 100) increased from £71 million in 1961 to £172 million in 1976.[6] This figure excludes television rental which more than doubled during that period. In 1976, 72 percent of households owned a washing machine, 88 percent a refrigerator and 95 percent a television set.[7] These figures show a remarkably complete penetration of a market that was only created in the 1950s.

The process of socialization of any particular part of domestic labor seems to follow a fairly constant pattern. In the first stage, the "need" it meets is one that has only been satisfactorily met in the homes of the bourgeoisie, often on the basis of the labor of domestic servants. It is thus seen as a "luxury." As mass production develops, it becomes cheaper and thus accessible to better-paid members of the working class. It is welcomed as evidence of increasing living standards, and more and more people aspire to owning it. In the next stage, it becomes essential—not just because of pressure to "keep up with the Joneses" but because social services and other facilities begin to be provided on the assumption that everyone possesses it. For example, houses are now designed so you have to have a refrigerator, as there is no other place to keep food cool; the next generation of schoolchildren will take examinations based on the assumption that they own pocket calculators. Thus workers, through their consumption needs, are tied even more closely into the wage system.

Another tendency is for the new jobs created by the manufacture of the new commodity or provision of the new service to be filled by women. This is not surprising when we consider that, on the one hand, capitalists will always seek out the cheapest possible source of labor, and on the other, the work will be closely associated with what has previously been seen as "women's work" in the home. What is surprising is the astonishing persistence of this pattern and the near universality of its application.

A quarter of all women employed outside the home are in occupations where over 90 percent of the workforce is female: typists, secretaries, maids, nurses, canteen assistants, sewing machinists. Another half work in occupations that are over 50 percent women: restaurateurs, cooks, kitchen maids, bar staff, office cleaners, hairdressers, launderers, clothing makers, waiters, housekeepers, social welfare workers, knitters, primary and secondary school teachers, electrical assemblers, textile workers, packers and labelers, telephone operators, and office machine operators.[8]

Nearly all these jobs bear a fairly obvious relation to housework or to the manufacture of household commodities. They are also poorly paid in comparison to men's jobs.

It seems likely that a similar pattern will follow the introduction of microprocessor technology: new commodities and services will emerge, which socialize new parts of domestic labor, deskilling housework still further; investment in existing services and manufacturing processes will lead to intensified exploitation of the workforce and more centralization, which will lead to the unloading of time-consuming and labor-intensive tasks onto the consumer; the increasingly stressful and unpleasant nature of paid work will thrust upon women an even greater demand to provide emotional support, peace, happiness, and pleasure; pressure to consume will intensify; new, poorly paid jobs will be created for women.

While it is too soon to make categorical statements, an examination of the existing evidence does seem to bear out certain patterns. Microprocessor technology has already generated new commodities. Ian Barron and Ray Curnow have this to say:

> In the short to medium term, many home devices, from television to cookers, may be expected to incorporate microcomputer controls. Such products will be developed independently by separate manufacturers and will be conceived as free-standing services unable to intercommunicate, except with a human controller. In the longer term, when a home information-distribution system emerges, it may be expected that various household devices will be developed to access and transmit information through the distribution system, so that, for example, the cooker

can be turned on remotely by telephone, the gas meter can be read remotely, and the television can be piped around the home.[9]

Microprocessor controls are already incorporated in some existing domestic products, and under development for others such as automatic dishwashers, cookers, microwaves, ovens, food mixers, sewing machines, power tools, alarm clocks, and cameras. There are also entirely new commodities, such as pocket calculators and video games made possible by microprocessors. Already, in Japan, the existence of TV games has created social change—amusement parlors with "space war" TV games have sprung up everywhere and become addictive among adolescent boys, who resort to mugging and house-breaking to raise money to continue playing. A visit to any seaside resort in Britain reveals how rapidly they are becoming established there.

Household robots incorporating microprocessor controls are being developed by several companies and can perform such tasks as scrubbing, sweeping, polishing, and vacuum cleaning. One, described in an article in the Guardian (12 December 1978) costs around £2,000 and comes complete with a skirt, "made small," say Quasar Industries, "so as not to be dominating." Domestic computers of various types are under development or already in prototype, as are a wide variety of electronic toys.

Microelectronic technology has also already led to the rationalization of service industries, with a corresponding increase in "self-service." As is described more fully in later chapters, the greatest impact of microprocessor technology is on routine, information-handling jobs in the service sector and the "service" parts of manufacturing. Much of the "saving" in this type of work is in fact passed on to the consumer.

To the extra time, expertise in operating machines, and carrying work foisted onto the consumer by these developments in self-service must be added the frustration of interfacing with machines and suffering the rudeness of the deskilled, unsatisfied bureaucrats who will become the only human point of contact between the consumer and most organizations.

As with other new technologies, microprocessor technology has had the effect of making most work processes more boring, stressful, unsatisfying, and alienated. Deskilling, machine monitoring, and increased pace of work all contribute to these effects, which result in physical and psychological symptoms with which the worker's "personal life" is supposed to cope.

Additional disruption of social and sexual life results from shift working, a form of working likely to increase with the introduction of this new technology, as managements try to get their money's worth out their investment before it becomes obsolete.

While women continue to be seen as responsible for family happiness and peace, the burden of coping with these tensions and providing the "pleasures" that are supposed to buy contentment will fall squarely on them.

Finally, the new technology has brought forth new low-paid jobs for women. As Rachel Grossman says:

> Competition in the [semiconductor] industry is still so heated that prices for its products are failing faster than the cost of production. In the race to survive, companies have introduced new products, such as electronic toys and home computers, while cutting costs in every feasible way. Since, ironically, much of the production process for the labor-saving devices is extremely labor-intensive, labor costs have been the major target for economizing.

The U.S. multinationals described in Grossman's article have scoured the world for the cheapest possible source of docile labor, and have come up with young Muslim girls in Southeast Asia, who, according to Grossman, can be employed for as little as 40 pence a day in appalling conditions— conditions that destroy their eyesight in four years, making them unemployable, except as prostitutes. Their work is assembling microchips. She goes on to describe how

> Asian electronics workers share much more than they know with their Californian co-workers. Approximately 60,000 assemblers work in the plants of Silicon Valley to begin the semiconductor production process and to test the finished products after Asian assemblers have completed their work. Ninety percent of these American workers are women, and roughly half of them are Asian and Latin origin, including Philippinians, Koreans, Vietnamese, Mexicans, Azoreans. Unlike their Southeast

Asian sisters, many of the women in California plants are single mothers who provide their families' primary support.

This development, reminiscent as it is of developments in the textile industry in the early nineteenth century seems to be just a foretaste of things to come. There is already evidence that British electronic components manufacturers are transferring production to third world countries, such as Malaysia, but it is likely that some production will be retained in the more "politically stable" industrialized countries. What seems clear is that the jobs created will be for the cheapest and most dispensable workers in our society—women, and more particularly, disadvantaged women: immigrants, single parents, and others who have no choice but to accept whatever work is offered to them.

It seems possible to draw several tentative conclusions from the above analysis. Firstly, it has become apparent that socialization of domestic labor does not in itself bring about women's liberation. Just as paid workers have discovered that socialization of the means of production does not liberate them from oppressive and alienating conditions of work, and have begun to demand workers' control over the work process as a means to liberation, so women must demand some form of control over the means of consumption, and of service, to be liberated from the oppressive and alienating conditions of domestic work. New technology is capital's instrument for bringing more and more areas of our lives within its orbit, but unless its control is challenged—not just at the point of production—it can only lead to intensified oppression. In other words, there are implications for the demands we make—inside and outside the workplace.

Secondly, there are implications for the way that we organize. New technology does not just affect paid work, it will also drastically change the nature of life in the home and in the community, and demands organization in the women's movement and in the community organizations to counter its worst effects. It seems possible that developments brought about by the technology itself might bring about the preconditions for new ways of organizing in the community. As its introduction in the highly automated industries tends to atomize workers and isolate them from one another, it also tends to herd consumers and users of services together—in queues, waiting rooms, etc. New types of agitation and organization may emerge in these conditions. Joint action between workers' organizations and community-based groups also seems possible. Such action has already taken place in limited ways; for example, hospital workers and users have taken joint action around hospital closures; bus workers and users against fare increases; tenants groups have come together with trade unions in Local Authority Direct Works Departments.

Finally, attention must be focused on the position of low-paid women workers in the new industries. They are at the receiving end of the worst effects of the new technology, both as unpaid domestic workers and as super-exploited paid workers. Unless action is taken to improve their position, conditions will be worsened for all women, and all paid workers.

/ 2 / DOMESTIC TECHNOLOGY: LIBERATOR OR ENSLAVER?

IT IS A TRADITION AMONG MARXISTS, including many socialist feminists, to assume that new technology is basically a Good Thing. The argument, much simplified, runs something like this: Once upon a time, before capitalism was established, nearly all work (production and services) was done in the home, unwaged. Women were the property of their individual menfolk by whom they were oppressed, and workers were isolated from one another in their homes. Then along came the twin forces of progress, science and technology. One after another, the tasks that had been carried out in the home became socialized. Spinning, weaving, brewing, baking, doctoring, making soap and candles, even entertaining—all the traditional women's tasks became paid jobs outside the home, creating as they did so a new self-conscious working class that sold its labor for wages.

This process did not happen all at once, of course, but can be seen as a continual process, lurching forward in the fits and starts that have characterized capitalist development over the last two hundred years or so. In that peculiar amalgam of the moral and the "scientific" that permeates Marxist thought, this was seen simultaneously as both inevitable and a Good Thing. It freed women from the "drudgery of housework" and released them to become full-time members of the ever-expanding working class on the same basis as men. Thus placed, it was only a matter of time before they were finally liberated by a socialist revolution, which would bring about a society in which all domestic labor was socialized and private property and women's oppression simultaneously evaporated from the face of the earth.

Over the past decade, socialist feminists have challenged the traditional conception of science and technology in the workplace, arguing that science is not neutral, and that the effects of the introduction of new technology may not improve the quality of work but, by deskilling workers and instituting new control mechanisms, actually bring about a worsening of working conditions. (I am not talking here about the effects of new technology on numbers of jobs, which socialists have always recognized as destructive to the working class under capitalism.)

One area that has been neglected in this general reappraisal of traditional socialist tenets has been the effect of new technology on women's position in the home. Surprisingly enough, it still appears to be a generally held view among socialists that automation in the home (and, for that matter, other applications of science) is unproblematically a Good Thing, while for many socialist feminists the slogan "socialization of domestic labor" still stands, almost an article of faith, for one of our fundamental aims, and, further-more, one that distinguishes us from other, non-socialist feminists.

This chapter examines some of the traditional assumptions about tech-nology in the home, to see how they stand up to actual experience. It explores some of the contradictions in housewives' situations and looks at the implications for socialist feminist strategies around new technology.

Any investigation of the effects of new technology in the home has to start with the incontrovertible fact that the technology which has so far been introduced has failed to liberate women from the role of houseworker and from the reality of many hours of unpaid household labor.

Despite much liberal theorizing about the "symmetrical family" and changes in the boundaries between "men's" and "women's" work, in most homes housework is still seen as the woman's responsibility, and research on hours of labor in the home suggests that, if anything, the amount of time spent by the average woman on housework is actually going up: from around sixty hours a week in the 1920s to over seventy in the 1970s, and this during a half-century when there has been an unprecedented increase in the number and variety of "labor-saving" appliances, household chemicals, convenience foods, and so on. What can be the explanation for this phenomenon?

It appears that several different factors make a contribution to this state of affairs. The first of these is ideological. As pointed out in chapter 1, and as Barbara Ehrenreich and Deirdre English have shown in much of their work, ideological forces have been powerful in bringing about what they call the "manufacture of housework."[1] The education system, advertising, and the advice of "experts" in medicine and psychiatry have all combined to persuade women whose grandmothers made do with an annual spring cleaning that every corner of their home must be disinfected weekly or even daily, that clothes should be washed after each wearing, and that children will suffer extreme deprivation if not given undivided, continual attention. So well have they done their job that none of us is immune from the crippling guilt that comes from believing we have neglected a child, or put someone's health at risk by allowing germs to breed in our filthy kitchens.

A second factor is a direct consequence of the privatization of domestic life. Each housewife, isolated in her own home, duplicates the work of every other housewife, and requires her own individual washing machine, refrigerator, stove, vacuum cleaner, and all the other items that make up a well-equipped home, from lemon squeezers to deep fat fryers, many of which are probably out of use 95 percent of the time. There is thus no economy of scale, which is often the main saving that automation brings. Getting out the food processor, assembling the bits, dismantling it, washing it up, and putting it away again takes as much time whether one is cooking for two or twenty, and the same applies to hundreds of other operations that all women carry out separately.

The third factor, less obvious but perhaps even more pervasive in its effects, results from applications of technology and science elsewhere in the economy. As areas of paid work are automated and rationalized to maximize profits and efficiency and minimize labor costs, so more and more unpaid "consumption work" (as it has be been labeled by Batya Weinbaum and Amy Bridges) is foisted onto consumers—in other words, onto women as housewives.[2] Thus, since the beginning of the twentieth century a whole new range of self-service tasks has been added to the traditional responsibilities of the housewife. If someone is ill, it is no longer the doctor's paid time spent traveling to and from the home, but the patient's unpaid time, traveling to and from the clinic and, once there, waiting. The housewife is now expected to transport herself to the nearest supermarket, find the goods she wants, take them down from the shelves, transport them to the checkout, wait, and transport them home—nearly all tasks that used to be somebody's paid job. The increased size of supermarkets has meant that the distances to travel are much farther, which in turn has led to increased reliance on home storage of food in freezers, for example, so the retailing industry is even managing to transfer much of its storage costs onto the consumer. And, in a society in which unpaid work is equated with women's work, such self-service tasks (economist Jonathan Gershuny talks of a trend toward a "self-service economy") will inevitably fall preponderantly on women, thus reaffirming the low value placed on women's labor in the wider economy, in a self-confirming circle, perpetuating women's oppression in the home.[3]

The roots of the fourth factor that contributed to extra housework lie in the woman's role as caregiver. She is expected to take responsibility for the health and safety of the entire family in and around the home, more particularly that of children and aged or handicapped dependents. As paid workers have discovered, new technology leads to new hazards, and, as a result of the scientific and technological developments of the past century or so, the home and its immediate environment are now a death trap for anyone who is not able-bodied, quick-witted, and literate.

Perhaps the three most important technological developments of the twentieth century—the internal combustion engine, the many-branched growth of the chemical industry, and electricity—are also three of the greatest killers, as anyone who has had to keep a toddler safe will appreciate. Outdoors, the danger from traffic is a constant nightmare; indoors, poisonous chemicals are used for everything from cleaning the lavatory to keeping Mummy tranquilized, while sockets and trailing wires make every room potentially lethal. Safety advertisements on television and in clinics emphasize, with guilt-provoking detail, that it is mothers who are responsible when children are mutilated and killed, and it is actually a legal offense in many countries to leave a child alone. Child care thus has become a tense, fraught, twenty-four-hour responsibility, and again science and technology have added to housework with one hand, while seeming to lighten it with the other.

In any discussion of the disadvantages of the new technology or science, there is a danger of appearing to glorify some pre-technological past golden age. That danger exists as well in the discussion of housework. It is important to remember that it has always been hard and that technology has brought about advances for women in terms of reduced physical effort, more choice, and freedom from some types of diseases. But we must always remember that it is contradictory. Just as contraceptive technology has given some freedom of choice to women about whether or not to have children (although it hasn't brought about liberation from male domination of the female body) while also creating new health risks, so domestic technology has brought some advantages, though in no way bringing about liberation from housework.

In some ways, the effects of technology in the home parallel closely the effects of technology in the factory, as analyzed by Harry Braverman and his many followers, whereby workers' skills and knowledge are appropriated and then incorporated into the design of the machines. Just as skilled craftspeople, such as lathe cutters, suddenly find themselves needing only to know which button to press on the computer-controlled machine, so the housewife can now discard all her expert knowledge about, for instance, different methods of washing various types of fabrics, and need simply select the right program on her automatic washing machine. Similarly, cooking may become a simple matter of following the instructions on the packet; the only skill required is literacy.

Dependence on the "expert" is also increased. We no longer understand what things are made of and how they work. In the workplace, this leads to a polarization between the few high-status jobs at the top and the many unskilled jobs at the bottom. In the home, women experience increased helplessness and dependence. When the warning on the aerosols says, "Caution, do not use near pets or foodstuffs; keep away from children," the homemaker has no alternative but to follow the directions slavishly, abandoning any possibilty of creative improvisation with the materials to hand. She also spends ever-increasing amounts of frustrating time waiting for the "expert" repairman or installer.

The effects of all this are very contradictory. On the one hand, the fact that household tasks have become easier and less specialized means that anyone can do them. This opens up possibilities of men taking a larger share in housework and potentially liberating women. On the other hand, it also gives men a greater confidence to criticize when work does not come up to the standards the advertisers claim for their products. The mysteries once handed down from one woman to another are now common property and no longer command respect. For older women in particular, this can lead to a feeling of dispensability and interchangeability with other women, which results not in greater liberation but in increased economic insecurity. This closely parallels the experience of older skilled industrial workers who feel themselves devalued and redundant when their jobs become easier as a result of new technology.

There is another sense in which these developments adversely affect women economically. A fully operating home these days requires a much bigger capital investment than in the past, and while most women earn little more than half men's wages, this can mean that a woman who decides to leave her man and set up on her own is plummeted into quite extreme deprivation, moving as she does from the standard of living of a one-and-half income family to that of a half income one. As society is increasingly reorganized on the basis that every normal household is equipped with a telephone, refrigerator, television, and many other appliances, surviving without these things becomes increasingly intolerable.

What are the implications of all this for socialist feminists?

In our personal lives, many of us find livable solutions—we live collectively with other women or cheaply on our own, push men into doing their share of housework, or find sufficiently well-paying jobs to buy our way out of the worst problems (though we often pay a price for this in perpetual exhaustion or enforced childlessness). When it comes to formulating demands to benefit all women, things become more problematic.

Clearly, it is not enough to take on new technology just in the workplace. We must recognize that it affects every other area of our lives, too, and find ways to resist its worst effects. Community organizations might provide part of the answer.

Perhaps we should start demanding more home visits from doctors, welfare officers, and midwives, or delivery services from supermarkets. We should definitely continue with campaigns for day-care facilities for children, the aged, and the handicapped, and for safer streets and play areas and better designed housing.

We must also, I believe, clarify what we mean by the socialization of domestic labor. It is possible to imagine a society in which just about all the things now done by women in the home are automated or carried out as paid services without capitalism having been dislodged or women achieving liberation. We must start defining what sort of services we want and insist that they are brought under our control.

/ 3 / TERMINAL ISOLATION: THE ATOMIZATION OF WORK AND LEISURE IN THE WIRED SOCIETY

THE HOME IS A SUBJECT THAT HAS RECEIVED little serious attention in recent socialist thought. Implicit in most arguments is a notion that the home is a space somewhat apart from the mainstream of economic activity, with internal social relations that are relatively autonomous and an economic role that can be simply and straightforwardly encapsulated in the single word *consumption.*

When this notion has been challenged, it has generally been by feminists, who have demonstrated the importance of the home as the site of the reproduction of labor power and the formation of gender relations. They have insisted that it is only in relation to the "private" social relations of the home that it is possible to understand many features of the "public" world, such as the occupational segregation of women in the workplace and the role of male violence in enforcing female compliance with a patriarchal order. Such theorizing, most of which has been directed toward developing an understanding of patriarchy in the totality of its relationship with capitalism, has inevitably concentrated on those aspects of home life that appear to be most universal; the theorizing has lacked historical specificity. Thus many of the changes that have taken place in the relationship between the home and the rest of the economy, and in its internal structure, have passed almost unrecorded. Without an understanding of these changes, it is difficult to grasp the impact of information technology on home life.

It is the purpose of this chapter to examine some of these developments, to look at the growing importance of the home as the locus of profound shifts in the boundaries between what is "public" and what is "private," and to examine some of the effects of information technology on the home. Without a clear analysis of the home, and political strategies based on such an analysis, socialist policies seem doomed to failure. Needless to say, an essay like this cannot provide such an analysis; it can merely sketch in some of the features it would incorporate. If it makes a contribution toward opening up a debate among socialists on the role of the home, it will have served its purpose well.

Before examining the effects of information technology on home life and their political implications, I should like to outline some of the other changes that have been taking place in the home, which set the context for the present upheaval and those predicted for the future.

POLITICAL ECONOMY OF THE HOME

Perhaps the most obvious and best documented of these changes has been the huge growth in owner occupation, given an added impetus in Britain by government policies. It was recognized at the beginning of the twentieth century—by the philanthropist and capitalist Andrew Carnegie, among others—that a working class that owned its own housing was the best possible protection against strikes and uprisings.[1] But such changes in political attitudes are not the only result of home ownership. Besides creating a vested interest in the status quo, greater dependence on a regular source of income, and a habit of hoarding, home ownership also has the effect of reducing mobility for whole households and for individuals within them. The mortgage can often be a more effective bond than a marriage license in cementing people to each other and to particular locations. As the supply of rented accommodation deteriorates in both quality and quantity, home ownership increasingly becomes a compulsory requirement for those seeking reasonable security and value for money.

Parallel with this compulsory investment in bricks and mortar goes another requirement, the result of major changes in the structure of industry outside the home. This is the necessity to invest in a whole range of capital goods, from cars to washing machines. These goods can be seen as the results of the process whereby service industries have been progressively commodified and their products individualized. This process has been chronicled by Jonathan Gershuny, who has shown how over the past three decades private forms of transport have been substituted for public ones, washing machines have ousted laundry services, and the purchase of television sets has replaced visits to the cinema or live entertainment.[2] As these new commodities have spread, use of the older services they replace has become relatively expensive, and they have tended to diminish in importance. We have thus increasingly been left with the choice of buying or doing without. The working class could, in fact, be said to be required to invest in its own means of reproduction to an ever greater extent.

The substitution of the purchase of commodities for the hire of services also has the effect of substituting the unpaid labor of the consumer for the paid work of the service worker, and creating a number of new tasks connected with the purchase, operation, and upkeep of these domestic appliances. Other aspects of the rationalization and automation of services also produce new types of unpaid work that the consumer must carry out, in the form of self service. Where services have traditionally involved labor-intensive interaction with the public by service workers, this has become the norm in recent years in a range of industries, including retailing, catering, banking, transport (gas sales, ticket dispensing), and various comparatively new forms of information retrieval. In the guise of "do-it-yourself," self-service has also replaced traditional crafts, such as cabinet-making, and trades like painting and decorating, while giving rise to profitable new industries manufacturing the tools and products that make such deskilling possible.

Again, it is comparative cost advantage that has pushed consumers into choosing these self-service forms over their traditional counterparts, based on the waged labor of large numbers of service workers or tradespeople. The older service forms have in most cases come to appear anachronistic—either luxuries for the rich or inefficient and wasteful methods reserved for those without the ability or wit to service themselves. In many cases, of course, the traditional forms were never within the reach of large portions of the working class, and the rise of self-service is perceived as raising their standard of living, bringing new comforts and status symbols within their grasp.

We can see that these processes have together resulted in a radical change in the job description of the consumers, or "consumption workers," as they have been more accurately designated by commentators such as Batya Weinbaum and Amy Bridges.[3] As some traditional tasks have been automated and deskilled, numerous new ones have been added, many of them formerly the province of paid service workers ranging from delivery boys to laundresses, from bank tellers to plasterers. These tasks are carried out singly and in isolation. They generally involve the use of technology or chemical substances whose workings and effects are not understood by their users. Housewives are then placed entirely in the hands of the "experts" when it comes to utilizing them. The labor process is thus increasingly controlled by the designers and manufacturers of these commodities, by means of fine-printed instructions which are disobeyed at the user's peril, with standards set by advertisements, and by less overt ideological pressures. (See chapter 2 for details.)

As consumption work becomes more private, and more and more of the energies of consumption workers are directed toward the improvement, maintenance, and protection of their individual homes and possessions, there is an accompanying erosion of public, collective forms of service. The pub, the cinema, the football stadium, the political meeting room—all have seen a spectacular drop in attendance over the past few decades. So too have a huge range of small businesses such as cafés, corner grocery shops, and high-street hardware stores, ousted by giant chains of fast-food outlets, supermarkets, and do-it-yourself shops that rely on self-service to keep their costs low. As workplaces, they have changed spectacularly, increasingly providing only employment that is casual, deskilled, and machine-paced, closer to factory work than to the old-fashioned service work that was characterized by a more leisurely pace, specialized skills, and a high degree of personal interaction with customers. From the customer's point of view, the changes are perhaps even more far-reaching, for these places represent the only spaces (outside their own workplaces, if they are fortunate enough to be employed in a collective space) where they can come together to exchange news and views, and develop an alternative interpretation of their daily experience from that handed down by the media. As any community activist will testify, encounters in public laundries, local shopping precincts, pubs, and the like have been crucial to the development of campaigns such as those to improve housing or oppose dangerous traffic schemes. At the more general level of the formation of political attitudes, it seems likely that they are also important. The general election of 1983 was widely experienced as the first almost exclusively "media election" in the United Kingdom, and it can be conjectured that the decline of public meetings, both formal and informal, played a part in Labor's crushing defeat. As public space is eroded and replaced by privatized activity, there is a corresponding loss of such alternative culture.

So far, I have discussed the changes taking place within the home as though they are gender-neutral in their effects. This is, of course, far from being the case. Most consumption work is done by women, who are disproportionately affected by these changes.

Where traditional domestic skills are disappearing, they are generally women's skills, but the skills involved in designing and repairing the new household technologies tend to be held fairly exclusively by men. Thus the new technologies can be seen, not as liberating women, but as providing another means whereby male power over women's domestic labor is reinforced, analogous to the control over women's bodies that medical technology has given to a largely male medical profession. Women also are the main sufferers from the increased volume of domestic labor and its redefinition to include new consumption-related tasks.

Finally, we must note the effects on women of the erosion of public space. This has several dimensions. Firstly, most women are considerably poorer than men, either economically dependent on them or subsisting independently on wages that are much lower. They are thus much less likely to be able to afford to purchase private alternatives to inadequate public services, such as cars, telephones, or video recorders; hence they are more severely incapacitated by the loss of community facilities. Secondly, women are the main caregivers, more likely to be tied to the home and neighborhood all day by the need to care for young children, or aged or handicapped dependants. Thirdly, women and children are most vulnerable to the increasing physical dangers present in the environment. Today, many children must play indoors for fear of traffic, just as their mothers and older sisters are confined to the house at night by the threat of rape. The absence of safe collective space, policed by the presence of neighbors, keeps many virtually imprisoned in the isolation of their homes.

STRUCTURE OF EMPLOYMENT

To understand the full force of the effects information technology will have on women's lives in the home, it is also necessary to take a more general look at the changes that have been taking place in relation to women's position elsewhere in the economy.

The postwar period has witnessed a large and unprecedented influx of women into the labor market. In particular, women, many of them working part-time, were the majority of those who flooded into the expanding service industries, so that by 1980 they formed over 40 percent of all workers in employment, with over a third involved in clerical work of some description.[4] During this period there has been a decline in the family wage, and most households are now dependent on female earnings to maintain themselves above the poverty line.

Women have also come to expect to earn an independent income during most of their adult lives. However, since the mid-1970s the concept of a woman's right to work has come under attack from several quarters. Cutbacks in public expenditure have removed many of the facilities, such as nurseries and day-care centers for the elderly and handicapped, which enable caregivers to go out to work. Changes in employment protection legislation have taken away many rights, particularly for part-time workers and those employed by small firms, in relation to maternity and protection against unfair dismissal. In addition, for the first time since the 1950s there has been an ideological onslaught on working mothers. Revamped theories of maternal deprivation and the doctrine of "community care" have meshed with the more traditional notion that male unemployment can be solved by women's return to the home, to produce a climate of opinion in which it is increasingly difficult for women to fight for their jobs. For example, right at the beginning of the Thatcher government in 1979, Lord Spens, opening a debate in the House of Lords, said, "If women could be persuaded to stay at home—especially those with children—that would provide a solution." He added, "I am not saying that they should not be occupied—just that they should not compete in the market for paid jobs."

And it has been during the same decade that women's jobs themselves have been increasingly under threat, partly as a result of the public spending cuts that have placed many service jobs in schools and hospitals at risk; partly through the general effects of the recession and the international restructuring of industries like electronics, textiles, and clothing, which have traditionally been major employers of women; and partly through the effects of information technology, which is being introduced into precisely those areas where most women work—shops, banks, and offices. Already this technology has radically transformed skill requirements in these industries, and introduced machine-pacing, stress, and a number of new health hazards associated with continuous screen-watching.[5]

The new technology has also brought about some job loss, though so far not on the scale predicted in the late 1970s when many commentators forecast that over a third of information-processing jobs would disappear as a result of new technology. The reason for this is not, in my view, that these forecasters were wrong. Rather, we have so far witnessed only the first stage of what is essentially a two-stage introduction of information technology. In the first stage, the key technology is that of microelectronics, with its capacity to cheapen and miniaturize, so that computing power can be widely introduced into information-processing functions that have previously been executed manually, perhaps with mechanical assistance. This stage is already well under way and has resulted in a proliferation of small, disparate computing systems: here a word processor, there a microcomputer, there again a computerized control system. It is rare for these systems to be interconnected, and most information still passes from paper into electronic form, and back into paper again during its useful life.

Stage two of the introduction of information technology depends much more heavily on telecommunications technology; it largely consists of connecting all these separate systems up to one another. It is only when this has occurred on a wide scale that the major productivity increases will take place, since it is only at this stage that the labor-intensive paper-processing phase of information handling can be eliminated. Already there in embryonic form in many industries, it is this telecommunications-based wave of technological change that is about to break over us.

TRANSFER OF WORK TO THE HOME

The effect of the new, cheap telecommunications data links will not just be to cause redundancies; it will also bring about fundamental changes in the location of information-processing work. With cheap methods of transmitting digital information, whether by cable or satellite, distance ceases to be an important factor in the location of terminals in relation to their parent computers. Information can be input or retrieved wherever it is convenient to site a terminal and its operator. This could be a distant office or the worker's own home. It is this fact, more than any other, that underlies the often-repeated statement that information technology is "good for the family." It is seen, quite simply, as providing the means whereby women workers can be returned to the home, and to the dominion of their husbands, without the loss of their services as a cheap form of clerical labor. This has been made explicit in many public pronouncements. For example, the invitation to a conference held in May 1984, organized by the Housing Association Charitable Trust, entitled "Planning for Homework" and addressed by planners and industrialists, enthused about the way homeworking would "restore the headship factor" to families.

Consider the scenario: there are in Britain upward of three million women clerical workers, of whom many have children and many have been trained to work with video display units and keyboards. While increasing numbers are being expelled from their jobs, few have access to alternatives, or to facilities that would enable them to seek them. Yet their need for an independent income has never been greater, because of rising male unemployment and cutbacks in social security benefit levels. From the employers' point of view, there is a need to cut costs and a strong trend toward casualizing the workforce wherever possible. The employment of homeworkers saves on overheads such as city-center floor space, sick pay, holiday pay, and pension schemes. It is also an effective means of preventing unionization and keeping wage levels as low as possible. The increasing home-centered nature of most people's lives and the deterioration of public transport and child-care facilities give an added incentive to such developments, with the final shove a psychological one, coming from the increasing hostility directed at women who go out to work and abandon their children.

These factors underlie the numerous forecasts of massive increases in homeworking by the 1990s. In purely physical terms, the ground seems well prepared for an increase in new technology-related homeworking in Britain. We have one of the highest per capita ownership of personal computers in the world; a population largely concentrated in dense easy-to-cable clusters in metropolitan areas; a government that has rushed through plans to cable the country on terms extremely advantageous to private industry with indecent haste and is now trying to sell off the national telecommunications grid at a knock-down price. Britain is a world leader in "viewdata" technology, which provides one way that such remote working can be carried out; one U.K. company, Rediffusion Computers, is already manufacturing "teleputer" workstations for precisely this purpose.

Yet all is not progressing quite as this outline might suggest. Investment in cable has not been as readily forthcoming as was anticipated. Mercury, the private telecommunications company set up to compete with British Telecom, is in deep financial trouble, with no prospect of any worthwhile return for its investors for a decade. Many of the companies that put in bids for local cable franchises in 1983 seem to have got off to a bungling start, unable to put together packages that appeal to their potential advertisers.

Meanwhile, interactive services are creeping into British homes under different guises. After a number of false starts, the BT Prestel "viewdata" system is making some headway, although a high proportion of its users are businesses. One scheme based on it is the Nottingham Building Society's "Homelink" service, which combines the Prestel information service with a home banking service. As an incentive to potential users, the hardware is available free to those with an investment of over £1,000 in the Building Society or a mortgage with the company, but some usage charges are still made, mainly to cover the comparatively expensive element of telephone time. A limited home shopping experiment has been set up in the London area for home-link subscribers, but this still seems to have progressed little further than as an amusing toy for the middle classes.

It is sobering to remember in this context how rapidly other products, such as video recorders, have progressed from this status to becoming an accepted part of the equipment of working-class homes. Nevertheless, it seems likely that the high cost of telephone connection, and the labor-intensive nature of the delivery services that must accompany home-based shopping, will be real brakes on the progress of this development. One home- shopping experiment in Gateshead relies on subsidies from the local authority and the Manpower Services Commission to sustain its ordering and delivery services.

Another factor that seems likely to hamper the progress of home-based interactive services stems from the very fact of the male domination of the design of the systems. In one Japanese experiment, in Higashi-Ikoma, a large number of services were made available for an experimental period between 2:00 P.M. and 6:00 P.M. on weekdays, and hence to a largely female, housebound audience. The system allowed for limited two-way communication, including the use of a video camera, so that users could transmit pictures of themselves or their children to other participants in the experiment. From the point of view of those who set up the experiment, it was a failure. There seemed to be little interest in using the information services provided, and a great reluctance to use any service that cost money (in line with the British experience of Prestel). What the system was used for, with enthusiasm, was to make friends. Having seen pictures of neighbors and their children on the television screen, women felt able to approach them in the supermarket and strike up an acquaintance. They were using the technology as a means to break down isolation and attempt to get out of their homes, rather than to stay in them, as the designers appear to have intended. The ability to do this was, of course, a direct result of the smallness of the experiment. The larger the number of people involved, the lower would be the chances of meeting someone seen on the screen.[6]

The results of this experiment give heartening evidence that many women will resist the introduction of systems that so clearly fail to address their needs if these systems are offered simply as entertainment or aids to home management. It seems likely in the long term, however, that other criteria will take over. The systems, like the present generation of home computers, will be purchased as toys for the male members of the household, aids to the children's education, or prerequisites for earning a living.

The other factor that complicates the simple scenario of work being transferred directly from offices into homes is the existence of satellite technology, which makes it just as easy to transport office work to other countries. Routine work, such as data entry, is already being shipped offshore by a number of U.S.-based companies, to sites where wages are a quarter of those of U.S. clerical staff. Sites chosen for this intensive, low-skill work are usually ex-British colonies in the third world, such as India and the West Indies, where English is spoken; but at least one company uses women in Ireland for long-distance office work. It seems likely that a situation will develop in office work very like that in traditional manufacturing industries relying on cheap female labor, such as the garment industry, where two workforces—homeworkers in the developed countries and third world workers based in sweatshops—are played off against one another by the employers.[7]

IMPLICATIONS FOR HOME LIFE

Whatever the exact time scale of these developments and the global breakdown of the division of office labor that results, it seems clear that the trend is overwhelmingly in the direction of casualization of labor and the reconstitution of the home as a work space. Taken together with the trends outlined at the beginning of this chapter, this represents a massive transfer of costs by capital onto workers, who now must bear not only many of the costs of what might be called the means of reproduction but also those of the means of production.

Workers are now expected to bear: the costs of house purchase and maintenance and interest charges on them; the cost of a range of capital goods to carry out the new domestic tasks that replace service industries (washing machines, electric drills, video recorders); much of the transport and storage costs of consumable products (trips to supermarkets, energy to run home freezers); the assembly costs of many consumer durables (self-assembly furniture, toys); the cost of a good deal of service labor (bank tellers, gas station attendants, shop assistants); the cost of some capital equipment necessary for paid work (industrial sewing machines, home computers, typewriters); and, increasingly, a wide range of overheads normally provided by employers—such as heating, energy, canteen, and floor space costs, and the costs of benefits such as paid holidays, sickness pay, maternity benefits, redundancy pay, and pensions—which most homeworkers are denied.

A superficial perusal of this list might suggest that such a development is progressive. Surely, one might argue, if workers now *own* all these things, then that gives them greater control over their living and working lives. Nothing, of course, could be further from the truth. All these developments are accompanied by a loss of control and a tightening of the leash by which workers are attached to capital.

This control is exercised in several ways. Firstly, it is strengthened by the atomization of the workforce. Isolated in their individual homes, it is increasingly difficult for them to combine to defend their interests, whether these are as consumption workers or as employees (or, indeed, in any other capacity—as women, as disabled people, as parents, as members of a specific ethnic group). Secondly, in relation to new technology for homeworkers, control is designed into the very form of the machines and systems used. It is now a standard component of any software package used for data entry, for instance, to closely monitor the performance of its operator, by counting the number of keystrokes per minute, the error rate, the number of items dealt with, the length and frequency of breaks, or any other variable useful to the employer. This can be used to police workers quite as effectively as many more traditional methods of supervision. Some companies have brought such remote control to a fine art, even exploiting the solidarity among workers in the drive to boost productivity.   One hire-purchase company operates a scheme whereby workers are monitored both as individuals and as work groups.[8] Only the latter records are made available to the women who operate the terminals processing loan repayments. The group that performs best over a period of time is rewarded by being given what is regarded as more pleasant work to do for a time—chasing up defaulting debtors over the telephone. Loyalty to other group members is the main mechanism that prevents slackening the work pace.

Even more sinister (if less direct) in its implications is a third form of control by individuals that information technology makes continually easier. This is the control that can be exercised through surveillance. The more functions are carried out from computer terminals, the more records of such transactions can be stored in easily accessible digital form. Already a bewilderingly wide range of records of individuals are kept by a variety of state and commercial agencies. Teleworking, teleshopping, and telebanking will add immeasurably to these, enabling more and more sophisticated portraits of individuals and their activities and predelictions to be built up. In the United States, homeshopping experiments are already being used to build "consumer profiles" of individual users, to enable advertising to be precisely targeted. Such data could as easily be used by the state to identify potential subversives or those involved in oppositional activities.

Big Brother, it seems, arrived right on schedule in 1984.

LEARNING THE LESSONS

What conclusions can be drawn from these tendencies?

First, it can be seen that workers are being dragged ever more firmly into dependence on a wage in order to support the investment that is now required in the fabric of their homes and the technology with which they must fill those homes. Lack of a wage creates increasing relative deprivation.

Second, there is a growing atomization of the working class, with an erosion of collective public space and of means of organizing and communicating. This strengthens centralized ideological control.

Third, women, far from being liberated by technology—domestic or otherwise—are thereby being placed into positions of greater dependence on men.

Fourth, despite a massive transfer of labor costs from service industries onto consumers and the growth of new forms of consumption work, a loss of control over the labor process of consumption work is taking place. This closely parallels the loss of control over labor processes in the workplace that automation brings.

Fifth, women seem likely to continue forming an ever-larger proportion of the paid workforce, but this role is increasingly likely to be carried out in the isolation of the home.

What are the implications of these developments for socialists and feminists? Perhaps the most important questions that arise are those relating to control: control of the design of technology and systems; control of the work process, be it paid or unpaid work; control of information; and control of the means of communication.

Control is an issue that has figured prominently in many recent debates on the Left. The experience of nationalized industries in Britain, for instance, has demonstrated that public ownership does not constitute public accountability or control. Women have learned that the existence of medical technology and drugs with the apparent potential for improving health has not given them more control over their own bodies but has, on the contrary, handed more power to the male-dominated medical profession. Similarly, workers' struggles over health and safety have taught the crucial importance of control over the pace of work in minimizing hazards. The spread of information technology raises similar questions; it gives an added urgency to the search for organizational forms and demands that will enable people to wrest back some of the control over their daily lives, which is increasingly being taken from them and placed in the power of the centralized institutions of capital and the state. Some existing activities point in this direction: popular planning policies like those of the Greater London Council; workers' struggles against casualization and for health and safety in the workplace; experiments in collectivizing domestic services; and campaigns against cutbacks in public services. However, it appears that few socialist programs address these questions in any systematic, large-scale way. In order to do so effectively, they must be rooted in a clear analysis of the effects of technological, social, and economic change—not just at the level of the state, region, or town, or of particular industries, but at the level of the individual home. It is in the home that Big Brother's power is most felt, in the helplessness that the single isolated woman or man feels when interfacing with his systems. Only when these mechanisms are fully understood can his power be combated.

/ 4 / THE GLOBAL OFFICE: INFORMATION TECHNOLOGY AND THE RELOCATION OF WHITE-COLLAR WORK

ALTHOUGH A CONSIDERABLE AMOUNT OF RESEARCH EFFORT has been devoted to studying the employment effects of information technology (IT) within the industrialized countries and to exploring its effects on skills and hence on the internal division of labor, comparatively little attention has been paid to IT's potential for enabling information processing work to be relocated, thereby contributing to an internationalization of the division of labor in white-collar work.

It is possible to identify three distinct though interconnected ways in which the introduction of IT has facilitated such a development.

The first of these stems from the "unbundling" or disaggregating effect of office automation on organizational structure. By formalizing decision-making structures and vastly increasing the potential for quantifying and monitoring the performance of each individual part of an organization, this has made a major contribution to the vertical disintegration of large organizations, leading to an increase in subcontracting and an expansion of small firms, particularly in high-technology industries. This trend cannot, of course, be viewed in isolation, and must be seen in the context of a general trend toward the casualization of employment that has also, in countries like the United Kingdom, been encouraged by government policies; for instance, by dismantling labor protection legislation and encouraging the privatization of public services. The vertical disintegration of industries has implications not only for the structure of employment within particular localities but also for the international division of labor. By making it much simpler than in the past to ship off individual fragments of the production process overseas, it has contributed to the deindustrialization of parts of the developed world and rendered much more complex the division of labor between developed and third world countries, which can no longer be analyzed in terms of a simple distinction between "head" and "hands."[1]

The second way in which IT changes the structure of employment is through its capacity for externalizing labor processes, and hence labor costs. This is particularly evident in (although far from exclusive to) service industries such as wholesale supply, insurance, and travel, where a central supplier serves a number of client companies. With the introduction of remote terminals in the offices of the client companies, it is possible for many routine clerical tasks formerly carried out at the central supplying organization to be carried out by clerical workers employed by the client organization, thus shifting a large portion of the labor costs downstream and changing the employment patterns of the industries and areas concerned.[2] Thus insurance companies have been able to shed labor at the expense of insurance brokers, tour operators at the expense of travel agents, car parts suppliers at the expense of garages and so on. In some industries like banking and branches of retailing, this process has already been taken to its logical conclusion by transferring much of the labor to the consumer, who carries it out unpaid on a self-service basis.[3] It should be noted that, because of the capacity of the computer systems to provide detailed monitoring and sophisticated management information systems, this decentralization of employment is usually accompanied by a centralization of control.[4] Needless to say, this development is not confined to decentralization within national boundaries but also has the potential for bringing about international shifts in employment.

The third way in which IT can bring changes in the pattern of work organization both within and between countries stems from its potential for enabling the introduction of "teleworking," or remote working using telecommunications links. This development is still in its infancy, and there are a number of problems, both technical and economic, to be overcome before it becomes widespread.

The technical problems are twofold. One prerequisite is the development of simple to operate but secure interfaces between the enormous variety of different computer systems currently in operation around the globe—in shops, offices, banks, government departments, factories, and homes. This requires the development of a considerable amount of complex software that does not yet exist. The second requirement is an extensive, international, cheap, high-capacity, interactive telecommunications network. This exists in part in the form of local cable networks, upgraded telephone grids, and satellites. However, coverage is patchy. This is partly because optical fiber technology, which could provide the basis for really cheap high-capacity local cable grids, is not yet sufficiently developed, and partly for economic reasons. It is likely to require large-scale state investment to develop this network to a point where it functions efficiently for mass teleworking in most parts of the world, an investment that, in the current political and economic climate, few governments seem inclined to make.

The fact that we do not yet have a universal interactive telecommunications system making electronic communications as cheap and accessible as computing power has become should not blind us to the fact that there is already a considerable, albeit limited, scope for teleworking that some organizations have already begun to use.

Within countries, this is taking several different forms, including the transfer of city-center jobs to suburban or branch offices and the increasing use of homeworkers for white-collar work, ranging from senior technical and executive jobs to routine data entry. This development has generally been accompanied by a lowering of wage levels and a reduction in job security and in sickness, holiday, maternity, and pension benefits for the workers concerned who—at least in the lower-skilled jobs—have predominantly been women tied to their homes by the need to care for young children.[5]

Internationally, there has been some transfer of technical work between countries using online telecommunications links. This has included the use of facsimile transmission to enable typesetting of newspapers to be carried out in one country while printing is done elsewhere; a specializing of certain data-processing functions in particular countries enabling, for instance, a database in Italy or the United States to be accessed from the other side of the world; and an increasing use of telecommunications for internal communications within large corporations, enabling different parts of a production process to be internationally coordinated. It is now possible for designers in one country to directly program production machinery in another. Most of these technical processes involve small numbers of staff, so that the net employment effect is not great, although the implications for control of production processes and for technology transfer are considerable. More important in terms of numbers of jobs affected has been the growth of offshore information processing, whereby satellite links are used to transfer routine data-entry functions to third world countries. U.S.-based companies, some of them specialist data-preparation subcontractors, are already known to be operating in this way in Barbados, Jamaica, Singapore, and parts of India for work involving the use of the English-language, and in Brazil and the Chinese mainland for number work. Generally the raw materials, such as airline ticket stubs, completed "special offer" forms from product packaging, or other labor-intensive routine paperwork are airfreighted out in large sacks to be keyed in by women working round-the-clock shifts on very low wages, in conditions that have earned their workplaces the epithet "electronic sweatshops." [6]

There are several points to be noted in relation to this development. Firstly, the work is of a low-skilled repetitive nature that brings neither useful skills nor any great financial reward to its practitioners.

Secondly, although it would be perfectly feasible for local entrepreneurs or co-operatives to set up as data-entry subcontractors, the evidence suggests that up to now it has been U.S-based companies that have dominated this field. Even with local ownership, autonomy would be difficult to achieve, given the high degree of centralized control that the online telecommunications link vests in the organization from which the contract originates. The computer systems used for data entry are capable of extremely sophisticated work monitoring, keeping records of the numbers of keystrokes per minute, error rates, numbers of items dealt with, and duration of work breaks of each individual worker, and comparing the productivity of one subcontractor with another, leaving little room for the development of more humane working methods and improved pay and conditions for the workers. Finally, it should be noted that this sort of work does not create permanent jobs. The need for bulk data entry is essentially transitional. The combination of increasingly sophisticated optical character recognition and voice recognition technology with the spread of user-friendly, online systems enabling users to access and input their own data is likely to make the job of the specialist keypunch or data-preparation operator obsolescent within the next decade.

In conclusion, it is clear that the development of information technology carries with it the theoretical possibility of bringing about a radical restructuring of information-processing employment, eliminating the need for most white-collar employment (and some manual employment related to computerized production and process-control systems) to be located in any particular place. This could bring with it a transformation of the existing unequal division of labor between developed and developing countries. In practice, however, unless there is a fundamental shift in the balance of power between transnational corporations and their workers and between developed and third world states, it seems unlikely that this potential will be realized. Rather, we are likely to see increasing centralization of control and the new technology being used as yet another instrument of dominance rather than a means to liberation.

/ 5 / CHALLENGING COMMODIFICATION—
PRODUCING USEFULNESS OUTSIDE
THE FACTORY

"PRODUCTION FOR USE, NOT PROFIT" has been a rallying slogan of socialists for many years. At first sight, it seems an excellent, concise encapsulation of what a socialist industrial strategy should be, simultaneously exposing the unfeeling nature of capitalism and demonstrating the sensible, caring quality of socialism. It has an instant appeal to common sense.

Yet, unpacked a little, the demand turns out to conceal a puzzling underlying contradiction, which exemplifies much of the current confusion by the Left about the direction an alternative economic and industrial strategy should take. For while it rejects the notion of profit as the overriding drive force of change, and as the ultimate criterion for whether or not a job should exist, it leaves unchallenged capitalism's favored form of industrial activity, chosen precisely because it is the most efficient way of producing profit—commodity production. Built into the very form of the capitalist manufacturing production process is the subordination of all other factors to profit, because it is only by manufacturing commodities for exchange that the capitalist can extract surplus value from the labor of his workforce.

The preeminence of commodity production has produced grotesque deformities in our industrial and economic development and brought into being many of the ugliest features of life under capitalism. It has meant that vast quantities of powdered cow's milk are available for babies, but there are no resources to educate their mothers to breast-feed them; that the provision of drugs or medical equipment takes precedence over the supply of nurses; that it is esier to find a miniature Rolls-Royce for a child than a nursery place; that we can equip old people with color televisions more readily than we can give them the warmth of friendship.

In an abstract, moralizing way, socialists have long been aware of the need for an alternative to this topsy-turvy value system, variously labeled as "materialism" or "consumerism," and have devoted much rhetoric to attacking it, generally in a tone of sentimental regret for the lost warmth of "close-knit" working-class communities before the Second World War. Yet when they come to the business of devising concrete plans for the future, the emphasis is firmly on alternative products. Although factory work is widely regarded as monotonous, deskilled, degraded, and dangerous, the solution proposed to the closing of factories is to reopen them or build new ones, not to think of alternatives to the factory system altogether. Why is it that the Left seems so reluctant to step outside capitalism's fixation with commodities? Why is the present socialist challenge to the primacy of profit so halfhearted and ambiguous?

A cluster of different, but related factors seems to be involved: the sexual division of labor that relegates women to the "service" jobs and leads to the perception that factory work is male; narrow and distorted definitions of skill that are the products of defensive struggles to sustain "craft" wage rates rather than any rational analysis of job content; a blind faith in science and technology as neutral heralds of a progress that will ultimately be beneficial to all; a belief that working-class consciousness and militancy are the exclusive preserve of operatives directly involved in the commodity manu-facturing process.

These attitudes have deep historical roots. Before going on to examine how justified they are, it may be a useful exercise to begin unearthing some of these roots, to see how they have come about and what their relationship is to the reality of the production process.

One starting point for this exercise, and the one adopted here, is to look at the processes by which various activities have become commodified over the past three centuries of capitalist development, and the effects that these processes have had on labor both within and without the cash nexus. It may then be possible to predict some future developments and plan strategies for intervention.

We are accustomed to a view of the economy that sees it as divided into distinct and separate sectors. There is the primary sector, consisting of agriculture, mining, and quarrying, in which raw materials are extracted from the earth; there is the secondary, manufacturing sector, in which they are turned into commodities; and there is the tertiary, or service sector, which comprises various state and commercial activities as well as a variety of distributive functions.

In addition to these three sectors of the money economy, there is a fourth group of activities, integral to their proper functioning but not involving waged labor. This has been called by a number of different names, none of them entirely satisfactory: the sphere of reproduction, consumption, domestic labor. It includes a variety of tasks carried out in the home and the community connected with the consumption of goods and services; with caring for the young, the old, and disabled; and with servicing the waged labor force. These tasks are predominantly carried out by women and, for the purposes of this chapter, will be termed unsocialized labor.

It is generally assumed that these four sectors of the economy are both discrete and constant, separated absolutely from one another by easily defined and unchanging boundaries, and these divisions are reflected in practices ranging from the routine collection of labor statistics to the formulation of political strategy. Whether it is the extreme right of the British Tory Party arguing that "we cannot continue to consume more than we produce" or the socialist Left bemoaning the "erosion of Britain's industrial base," the underlying assumption is the same: that it is possible to separate and counterpose the "productive" manufacturing sector and the "unproductive" services.

It thus requires quite an adjustment to recognize that the boundaries between these sectors are not only extremely blurred, but are also dynamic. Underneath the apparently static surface portrayed in the official statistics, there is constant movement, with shifts and upheavals which profoundly affect all our lives.

At the micro-level—that of the individual worker—it is easy enough to point to the blurring between sectors. A farmworker is mending his tractor—a "primary" activity. He fails and has to call in a service engineer to do the same job. Immediately it's reclassified as "tertiary." A typist is typing the manuscript of a book, and thus is employed in manufacturing. She is made redundant and reemployed in the civil service where she now types official reports, and she has become an unproductive service worker. The man carrying newly completed stainless steel forks across the factory floor is in manufacturing; the woman carrying them across the shop is in services. From accountants to lorry drivers to cleaners there are many large groups of workers whose classification is essentially an arbitrary by-product of the size and degree of specialization of their employers and whether or not there is a policy of subcontracting work.

While anomalies such as these serve a useful purpose in warning against overreliance on the available data, they tell us little about major shifts in the boundaries between sectors. To see these, we need a broad historical overview. Any summary of the past three hundred years of capitalist development in a few paragraphs is bound to be somewhat crude and simplistic. Nevertheless, it seems worth attempting for the light it sheds on the transformation of services into goods, and of unsocialized labor into paid work and back again.

At the beginning of this period, in the seventeenth century, the manufacturing sector as it is today hardly existed. Many of the activities that now take place in factories, as well as a number of those now labeled "services," took place in the home. Let us look again at the quote from Alice Clark used in chapter 1:

> In the seventeenth century it (the domestic role) embraced a much wider range of production: for brewing, dairy work, the care of poultry and pigs, the production of vegetables and fruit, spinning flax and wool, nursing and doctoring, all formed part of domestic industry.[1]

The range of goods produced in the home was immense, covering such items as soap, candles, and medicines, as well as food and clothing.

The first major production activity to move out of the home was textile manufacture, which, in the first factories, brought into being a new class of wage-earning workers. As the factories began to be established, and waged work outside the home was created for women, the effect was not, as one might expect, to enrich the household by providing a source of income with which the new factory-made goods could be purchased. Again to quote Alice Clark:

> If the father earned enough money to pay the rent and few other necessary expenses, the mother could and did feed and clothe herself and her children by her own labors when she possessed enough capital to confine herself wholly to domestic industry. The value of a woman's productive capacity to her family was, however, greatly reduced when, through poverty, she was obliged to work for wages, because then, far from being able to feed and clothe her family, her wages were barely adequate to feed herself.[2]

It seems to have been necessity, in the form of a shortage of time and financial resources, that fueled the choice to become a consumer of manufactured goods rather than to continue to produce them in the home. The new factory workers were also obliged by their lack of time and inadequate accommodation to become purchasers of services, a prerogative hitherto restricted to those rich enough to employ domestic servants. This gave rise to a new range of "service" occupations such as child minding, taking in washing, and purveying cooked foods, some of which were later to become the basis of major new industries.

Accompanying this development was a continuing growth of the professional services that had already begun to oust some of the functions previously carried out voluntarily in the community by wise women and respected elders—the fee-charging surgeons and apothecaries, doctors, and lawyers—and the replacement of oral traditions of education by literary ones.

Thus far, we have seen a movement of some activities out of the sphere of unsocialized labor and into that of manufacturing, and of others out of unsocialized labor and into that of services. But there is another type of movement, which became increasingly important over the succeeding centuries—a movement from services into manufacturing.

To illustrate some of these changes with concrete examples, we could choose from a large number of activities that were almost exclusively in the home in the seventeenth century: washing clothes, caring for the sick, entertaining, preparing food, supplying heat and light, passing on news, making clothes, or cleaning. Before the Industrial Revolution, each of these tasks was carried out mainly by women for the use of the immediate household. In addition, the labor process for each of the tasks required fairly high general levels of skill and knowledge. The pace of the work was controlled by the worker, and the entire work process and any hazards involved in the work were known and understood by the worker. For example, the activity of washing involved the care of personal and household fabrics and included washing, ironing, starching, soap making, and dry cleaning. Similarly, entertaining involved singing, storytelling, performing with musical instruments, and dancing.

Gradually, as capitalism took hold, many of these activities became transformed into paid, sometimes "professional" services which, although they may have already existed embryonically long before the Industrial Revolution, began to become widespread with the growth of wage earning. For example, we begin to see domestic service and outwork, such as taking in washing and laundry work. Or we see professionals entertaining in bands, orchestras, circuses, and music halls, as well as, later, working as projectionists and usherettes in cinemas.

In order for these tasks to move outside the home there was no necessity for the way in which they were carried out to change. The technology and work process remain identical, the only alteration necessitated being one of social relations—the performers of the tasks were now carrying out the service for money, not for their own use or that of their families. The next step, however, required the intervention of science and technology in order to take place. This was the transformation of these activities into manufactured ones, their "commodification," as one might call it. For the cleaning services sold in the market to generate the manufacturing of commodities such as soap, detergents, washing machines, and dryers, there had to be technological changes in the chemical industry and in mechanical and electrical engineering. Before there could be manufacturing of radios, records, televisions, hi-fi sets, and the like, technological changes involving sound and vision recording and transmission techniques, along with cables and satellites, had to occur. In the new manufacturing labor processes, a few skilled workers are needed, but most of the work is done by relatively unskilled operatives with little overall knowledge or control of the work and its accompanying dangers.

Finally, the new manufactured products gave rise to new consumption activities in the home or new forms of unsocialized labor: buying, operating, and maintaining appliances, purchasing or renting hardware and software. Here too skill requirements, overall knowledge, and control are low.

The overall pattern of development of all of these activities emerges as remarkably similar. The functions are initially socialized mainly as services that, as a result of technological change, are then commodified to provide the basis for new manufacturing industries. The existence of these new commodities in turn alters the consumption patterns of the mass of the population, transforming the nature of the remaining unsocialized labor. It would be wrong, of course, to imply that this development is a smooth and consistent one. It has come abut through a series of unsteady jolts, with long periods during which several stages of development exist alongside each other. However, since most "service" methods of production are more labor-intensive than "manufacturing" ones, they inevitably become more expensive in relation to the purchase of commodities as mass production gets under way and tend to dwindle into insignificance or survive as luxuries for the very rich.

Jonathan Gershuny has done pioneering research on this process whereby services are ousted by goods. His work gives us concrete information on the extent and time scale of such change, and demonstrates conclusively that, although invisible in conventionally assembled statistics, it is a sweeping trend with far-reaching implications. For instance, in one twenty-year period there was a complete reversal of the relationship between consumption of services and goods in three areas: the substitution of commodity-based entertainment for cinema and theater-going, the use of domestic appliances instead of laundry services and domestic help, and the use of cars and motorcycles instead of public transport.[3]

In the seventeenth century, a crucial factor in the choice to buy goods or services rather than produce them in the home was the shortage of time, as mentioned above. It would be reasonable to expect that there would

continue to be a direct relationship between the growth of socialized labor
and reductions in time spent on unsocialized work—the more that goods
and services were produced for household consumption, the less the time
needed to spend on housework. However, as we saw in previous chapters,
such has apparently not been the case. As Ann Oakley has shown, in the
twentieth century, during a period when there was an unprecedented and
spectacular proliferation of domestic appliances, household chemicals,
speedy forms of transport, and other "labor-saving" commodities, the time
spent on housework actually went up.[4]

We have discussed the reasons for this unlikely phenomenon: powerful
ideological pressures to force up standards of housework, the small scale of
each individual household that prevents economies of scale, and the above-
described creation of new types of household consumption activity. It is this
third reason that requires some additional discussion.

The commodification of services has had the effect of creating new types
of unpaid "consumption" work. It could in fact be said to have desocialized
many labor processes that previously constituted part of paid employment.
For example, in shops the consumer has taken over many of the tasks of
goods selection, transport, weighing, packing, and waiting that used to be
carried out by paid assistants. Self-service has also become the norm in such
services as gas stations, cash dispensing, and cafeterias. In health service, it
is no longer usual for doctors and nurses to visit patients in their own homes.
It has been discovered that their paid time can be saved if users of the services
can be persuaded to devote their unpaid time to traveling to and waiting in
clinics and outpatient departments of hospitals. Where computerized diag-
nostic systems have been installed, the patients also take over many of the
tasks previously performed by admissions clerks and nurses, feeding their
own details into the information system.

There is also additional labor involved in servicing and using many of
the new privately owned commodities, although this is often masked by the
apparently greater ease and convenience of owning your own machine
rather than relying on a public provision that has become expensive and
unreliable. It is, for instance, more time-consuming to do washing even with
an automatic machine than it was to use a laundry service which collected
from and delivered to one's front door.

Processes such as these represent yet another shift in the boundaries between socialized and unsocialized labor. The traffic between the private sphere of the home and the public one of the cash economy can now be seen as two-way. As more and more activities are pulled out of the home and socialized, the interests of forcing up productivity and shedding as many unprofitable tasks as possible in the outside economy are thrusting back on the consumer other tasks that add to the burden of unpaid labor. I alluded above to changes in the labor process that have accompanied these changes. Let me now provide some details. In the seventeenth-century household we find an extremely wide range of tasks, with seasonal variety, which, even allowing for an internal division of labor, demanded a broad range of skills from the workers. Most tasks were carried out from start to finish within the home, so all participants would have had an understanding of the total process and a high general knowledge of such things as cooking, curing meat, preserving methods, preparation of medical remedies, textiles, brewing, the manufacture of candles and soap, the caring of animals, and so on. While many individuals were overworked and bullied, the pace of work, except in unusual circumstances, must have been determined informally or by group pressure when not controlled by the individual.

Turning to the service industries, we find an enormously diverse range of types of work. However, it is possible to identify a characteristic type of "service" job. This is one in which the range of skills and knowledge is not so wide as in the unsocialized household work of the seventeenth century but has a greater degree of specialization, resulting in the development of a number of highly skilled occupations, each dedicated to one particular type of task. In medicine, for example, the "all-rounder" of the informal economy is replaced first by specialist pharmacists, surgeons, midwives, physiotherapists, gynecologists, ophthalmologists, and a host of other specialists.

This increasingly complex division of labor also resulted in specialist positions being created that do not involve such high levels of skill. These are mainly manual jobs, such as cleaning, carrying messages, and delivering goods, positioned at the bottom of the job hierarchies which quickly developed in these new industries, but with some worker knowledge of the work process as a whole. Most involve interaction with people, and forms of supervision and work pacing are determined by human beings rather than machines.

Many service industries have also provided some form of progression, with the possibility for workers to work their way up from subordinate to more senior positions. The combination of a high degree of specialized knowledge and a low level of automation has meant that most work hazards have been well understood, making avoidance relatively easy.

In manufacturing, the situation is very different. As many commentators have noted, the overall tendency has been inexorably in one direction—the incorporation of as much of the skill content and control of the work as possible into machines and systems and the rendering of the vast majority of workers into an undifferentiated, unskilled, interchangeable mass. In relation to skills, a dual process takes place: on the one hand, the creation of a few extremely highly skilled controlling and designing positions, and on the other, the development of a larger number of repetitive jobs each involving carrying out one small fragmented part of the production process. The gulf between the two is unbridgeable. Most workers now lack any overall view of the labor process and only fully understand their own small part of it. The chemicals with which they must work, the computerized control systems, and the other products of a mystified "science" have been made incomprehensible to them, which means that their hazards cannot be understood, either. Often, it is only when workers begin dying that any suspicion arises to their dangers. Work is paced by machines, taking from the individual worker not only the power to pace the speed of the job but even, very often, the ability to argue about it with a human supervisor.

What about the work carried out in the contemporary home? While the basic functions are, of course, similar to those carried out in homes three centuries earlier, the manner in which these functions are carried out is vastly different. It turns out, on analysis, that household consumption work bears great resemblance to the labor process in manufacturing just described. It is based overwhelmingly on the purchase, servicing, and use of various commodities such as processed food, household chemicals, domestic appliances, and manufactured clothes. The design and working method of most of these are not understood and the housewife must depend on the advice of "experts" (usually in the form of fine-printed instructions) for information on how to use them and what their hazards might be. In the event of any breakdown or accident she is instructed to contact other experts—the repairmen or a doctor—and must helplessly wait until they have put the matter to rights (if, indeed, they are capable of doing so).

The housewife does have some control over the order in which she carries out tasks within the tight time structures dictated by school, work, shop opening hours, and other external timetables, but the tasks she must carry out and the standards to which she must comply in doing them are increasingly determined by the design of machines and houses, the chemical composition of food mixes or fabrics, legal constraints (such as laws governing when children may be left with others or schooled), and strong ideological pressures. All of these mitigate against any real control of the work process. These processes have also removed most of the skill from housework, incorporating it, as in the case of factory workers, into the design of machinery. Is it any wonder then, as we noted in chapter 1, that in terms of monotony, fragmentation, and speed, housewives actually rated their work as worse than that of manufacturing workers?

Far from liberating women from housework, then, we can see that the increasing commodification of household and service activities has had the opposite effect, transforming it into stressful drudgery. It has had a similar effect on factory work, each wave of automation eliminating more skill and satisfaction from the work. The development of information technology has also had the effect of commodifying large areas of service employment, not only creating new manufacturing industries but also spreading some of the social relations of the factory into the office, shop, hospital, and bank. Fragmentation and machine pacing are now becoming characteristics even of some service jobs.

In the face of this knowledge, how can socialists argue uncritically for more commodification as a way of creating worthwhile jobs and a better society? Do they really believe that it is more pleasant to work in an electronic alarm factory than to sit and talk to a frightened old lady? Or to stand at a conveyor belt making trolleys than to help her carry her shopping? Is it really less rewarding to be a hospital porter or a nurse than a packer in a drug factory? And which of these jobs has the most potential for change, for transforming the social relations within an industry to give workers more involvement and control in their daily life?

As I observed at the beginning of this chapter, there appear to be several barriers in socialist thinking to developing strategies that challenge the primacy of commodity production.

The first of these is the sexual division of labor. In the unsocialized labor sector, it is overwhelmingly women who carry out the work of consumption, running the home and servicing the family. In the money economy, women are concentrated in relatively few industries and even fewer occupational groups. Apart from transport and defense, men are in a minority in all the service industries, which thus tend to be seen as female, while they dominate all the other industries with the exception of clothing and footwear, an industry closely associated with unpaid activities carried out by women in the home. Women also have a substantial minority presence in the food and drink industries, electrical engineering, and textiles, where they tend to be concentrated in certain clearly designated "women's" jobs, but elsewhere they are hardly present at all except as clerical workers or cleaners. Perhaps precisely because they are responsible for unpaid work in the home, women's time is not regarded as valuable, and these sharply differentiated areas where they work are generally also ghettoes of low pay.

Closely associated with this phenomenon is a devaluing of women's skills. A number of skills such as cleaning, cooking, child care, and making clothes are expected to be part of the normal equipment of every woman, who will, it is assumed, exercise them without reward for the good of her family in the home. They thus have no scarcity value whatsoever, so that when they come to be exchanged in the marketplace for wages, the price they fetch is rock-bottom. In fact, they are frequently not regarded as skills at all, and those whose livelihood depends on them are generally labeled "unskilled."

The question of how skills are to be defined is confused and emotionally charged, as Cynthia Cockburn has pointed out in her book, *Brothers*.[5] Frequently, the designation "skilled" attached to a job is not so much a reflection of the intrinsic difficulty of performing it as of the degree of organization and bargaining power of its holder. A central plank of the resistance of workers to the degradation and fragmentation of factory work has been the protection of past practices by labeling them "skilled" and controlling access to them through the creation of apprenticeship schemes and the like. One explicit purpose of these craft groupings has been to resist dilution by more vulnerable groups of workers such as women and immigrants whose presence might weaken their bargaining power and unity, thus perpetuating and reinforcing the division of labor referred to above. These practices have led to an identification of jobs done by women with low status. Most "service" jobs are regarded as menial and degrading, if not effeminate, not so much because of their intrinsic nature but because they have taken on the attributes ascribed to those who normally carry them out.

Alongside this distorted evaluation of the relative value of different types of employment, there is on the Left a stereotyped view of worker militancy. It is very difficult to shake off the idea that because it is the factory system that creates a class-conscious proletariat, it must therefore be here that strong workers' organizations will emerge which will bring capitalism to its knees. Leaving aside the role of peasants in Russia, China, Cuba, and other countries that have experienced revolutions, we need look no further than British history to see what a dubious proposition this is. By far the most powerful political force in the British labor movement in this century has been the so-called triple alliance of dockers, miners, and transport workers. Not one of these groups is involved in factory production. The miners are involved in primary sector extraction, and the other two are designated "service" workers. All three are, however, male, which may partly explain that they are not generally perceived as such. Not so the workers who brought down the British government in the "winter of discontent" in 1978. These were largely female public sector service workers. It is difficult to point to any group of manufacturing workers whose actions have had such great political effects, although it is certainly true that many have shown great militancy in pursuit of their aims as compared with some service workers. This would appear to be, however, not so much a product of their different relation to capital as of their gender.

Women service workers find it harder to organize not because they are service workers but because they are women: they cannot attend meetings because of household commitments; they are obliged to work part-time or for small firms near where they live; they are excluded, patronized, or harassed by men; or their economic need is too desperate to hold out for the best wages and conditions. These three factors are closely connected. Together, they give us a negative stereotype of which the positive mirror image is of the working-class militant as a white, male factory worker, whose work is somehow ennobling. As the only "real producer of wealth," his labor is not only seen as important and dignified but also as skilled and providing some sort of a model for how all work should be in a future socialist society. By contrast, other work—generally in services—is considered servile and undignified, if not downright parasitic. It is also perceived as unskilled and womanish, not fit employment for a real man.

Statistics show that the real composition of the working class contradicts this image. In Britain, over 40 percent of workers are women, and an even higher proportion of workers is employed in service occupations. But this image also sits uneasily with socialist ideology at a more abstract level. For we are, are we not, committed to trying to create a more caring society? And if caring is to be socialized, then what does it consist of but services? And how are we to fit this boiler-suited male factory worker into such a vision? The resolution of this contradiction is no simple matter, and it must have exercised quite a few minds on the Left over recent years. It is this dilemma that must explain the delight with which so many have seized on the idea of the alternative, socially useful product. For if such "alternative" products can be identified, then these workers can be put back into their factories and carry on exercising their skills while also producing the use values people need. They can show they care without ever having to contaminate their manhood by actually entering into a service relationship with the needy.

Such a solution also conforms with another idea commonly held among Marxists and which reinforces the idea that more and more commodity production is the way forward to a socialist future. This is the notion that science and technology are neutral forces of progress that must be developed as rapidly as possible so that, when the time is ripe, they can be appropriated by the working class under whose ownership they will produce leisure and plenty for all. In the past few years a critique of this idea has emerged, in Britain led by the women's movement and groups like the British Society for Social Responsibility in Science. Together with some trade unionists, ecologists, peace groups, and people involved in alternative health practices, they have developed a convincing analysis that portrays capitalist science as fundamentally distorted. The technology, in this view, is developed for destruction not construction; it is anti-woman and anti-worker in its conception and design and could not be taken over in its existing form without continuing to pose an enormous threat to life, health, and control of daily life. The science is mystified and irrelevant, its priorities dictated by the class that pays for and directs its progress. This critique gives us further grounds for caution in the face of the idea that more commodity production will necessarily take us a step toward socialism.

What, then, is the way forward? It is obviously misleading to suggest that there was a pre-technological golden age in the past during which people's lives were pleasant and healthy, and to which we should seek to return. New technologies have always had contradictory effects and have eliminated many evils, even as they have created new ones. The process of commodification is not in and of itself necessarily against the interests of the working class as a whole, or of women within it. However, it seems to me that it needs to be questioned much more carefully than it has been in the past by socialists.

When devising strategies for the future that seek simultaneously to create jobs and to meet social needs, the starting point should not be the assumption that a product will necessarily be the answer. If it is, then in all probability forces already at work within capitalism will find it. On the contrary, we should start from an analysis of the unmet need, which means listening to the views put forward by the needy themselves through their own organizations. Do childbearing women really want more fetal monitors, or would they rather simply have more, and differently trained midwives? Do the severely disabled want new gadgets, or would they prefer more money, more home aides, or differently designed houses? What labor does housework actually consist of, and how could it best be socialized? Can we reverse the trend toward a more capital intensive service sector and the self-service economy? And how can work processes be redesigned to make them safer and more satisfying? Some of these questions may produce answers that suggest new commodities are needed, but it is likely that a great many will not.

If we are to produce solutions that meet these needs without creating new ghettoes of poorly paid, low-status work, then a number of cherished ideas must be challenged and new ways of organizing developed. In particular socialists must begin to question the sexual and racial division of labor and find ways to overcome it, and begin to make it a priority to listen to and help organize groups that have traditionally been silent and isolated, in the community and in the unionized parts of the service sector.

/ 6 / WOMEN'S HEALTH AT WORK

IF WE TAKE THE WORD "HEALTH" TO MEAN more than just the absence of a medically diagnosed disease but a positive state of well-being, then we need some more general word than "disease" to denote its opposite—the state of "not-well-being." The original meaning of "disease" ("dis-ease") was much more general, as was that of "illness" ("ill" simply meaning the opposite of "well"). However, both these words have been so effectively hijacked to signify specific, medically recognized conditions that they have lost much of their usefulness. That there is a need for a more general term is clear from common speech. People talk about feeling "off-color," "peaky," "stressed out," "debilitated," "run down," "poorly," or, most tellingly of all, "not quite myself."

Simplest solutions often being the best, in this chapter I have chosen to employ the word "ill" in its original meaning of "not-well" and use the term "ill-being" to describe states like these that fall short of complete well-being while not necessarily fitting tidily into categories that can be accurately described in a single, multisyllabic phrase on a doctor's certificate.

This chapter, then, is about how waged work affects women's well-being, or produces ill-being, in the broadest sense, encompassing hard-to-define states of discomfort, stress, or misery as well as medically recognized diseases.

The first question to be addressed is: Why consider women separately from men at all? Surely, it might be argued, if a workplace environment is unsafe or a chemical hazardous, this is likely to affect human bodies equally, regardless of sex, and to treat women as a separate species is to obscure the real dangerousness of the situation. Is there not a risk that a focus on women as vulnerable will lead to discriminatory policies that exclude them from certain jobs altogether? This is a real danger, to which we will return. However, there are a number of good reasons, some of them interconnected, why it is impossible to understand health in the workplace without focusing separately on women.

The first, and most obvious reason is that women's bodies are different from men's in several ways. Women have breasts, vulvas, and uteri, while men have penises. Women menstruate, while men, although their moods and metabolism may also be subject to cyclical changes, don't. Women carry and give birth to babies; men don't. Women are, on average, smaller, lighter, and less strong than men, although the overlap between them is greater than the difference: Caucasian women, for instance, are often larger than Asian men; young women are stronger than old men, and so on. Differences in size and strength only matter because most current safety standards—such as exposure to certain chemicals or maximum permitted weights for lifting—are set on the assumption that the worker is a young, fit white man (in the United States, for instance, it is common to use "volunteers" from the U.S. Marine Corps for testing chemical exposure). Such standards put at risk anyone who is smaller, or whose susceptibility may be increased because of old age or disability.[1]

Some work hazards are directly related to women's distinctive biology. Until the Second World War, it was common for women in the Lancashire cotton factories to be refused permission to leave their machines except for certain short, set periods. So when they were menstruating they had to use whatever was available—usually an oily rag—to mop up the flow of blood. As a result of prolonged contact with the industrial oil, many developed cancer of the vulva. By a similar process, male garage mechanics are liable to contract cancer of the scrotum, from rubbing against oil-soaked overalls. However, the work-related origin of the women's genital cancer took much longer to be discovered, because, until very recently, women were recorded in the official United Kingdom statistics (*Standard Mortality Ratios*, which provide information on cause of death) under their husbands' occupations.

Menstruation is a touchy issue in the debates about equal opportunities.

Faced with gross discrimination, and employers keen to seize any argument to perpetuate it, the "equal rights" school of feminism has traditionally argued that its effects are insignificant. What business is it of the employer's, these women would argue, whether a woman is menstruating or not? Making this information public is not only an invasion of individual privacy, but also exposes women to a variety of forms of harassment, ranging from offensive jokes to religious taboos against men working alongside menstruating women. According to this approach, one's periods are a purely private affair, which do not impinge on work in any way.

Yet this belief coexists uncomfortably with another, often acknowledged in private conversations between women: that having a period can be painful (with stomach cramps, for instance, or premenstrual migraine attacks) and physically draining; and that it can make some people clumsier than usual or less able to concentrate.

In Japan, it is widely accepted that women will suffer when they are menstruating, and menstruation leave is a standard entitlement, and welcomed as a benefit by most working-class women. Their middle-class sisters are not always so sure. Using abstract arguments based on equality, many have argued that such "unequal" treatment can be used to justify giving men preferential treatment elsewhere in the workforce in debates echoing those that have rumbled intermittently for over a century in the West over whether women should be "protected" from night work, reproductive hazards, or carrying heavy weights.

For the individual woman, in her individual workplace, the situation is a no-win one, unless she has completely trouble-free periods or is well past her menopause. She has a choice of concealing her periods and pretending to feel better than she does, or of making them known and, if necessary, taking extra time off work, as a result of which she may become the butt of jokes and be treated as an inferior worker. Either option is stressful; neither is conducive to well-being.

In a more extreme form, the arguments about menstruation are reenacted around pregnancy and child bearing. The fight to protect a woman's right to retain her job during and after childbirth has been so hard fought that it has been difficult to raise specific demands for extra provisions to protect health during pregnancy. Here, a central difficulty has been to distinguish between the health of the fetus and the health of the mother. The traditional view, reinforced by employers and their insurance companies (terrified of being sued for damage to the fetus), has been to prioritize fetal health and to treat the mother simply as a fetus carrier who constitutes a hazard to her unborn child just by working at all. The logic of this argument requires that, at any hint of danger, the pregnant woman, or even, in some circumstances, the woman who may at some future date become pregnant, should be excluded from the workplace altogether.

Such arguments ignore the fact that anything that damages a fetus (such as lead or ionizing radiation) is also likely to damage any adult human being, male or female, and is often used as a smokescreen by employers anxious to avoid cleaning up the workplace. Once women of childbearing age have been excluded, men—often paid extra money for the risks they are running—remain working in highly dangerous environments with no concern for their health or that of their unborn children (both radiation and lead also adversely affect male fertility). That such measures have not really been taken for the benefit of women and children becomes clear when one examines the unconcern with which women are exposed to the same hazards in other contexts—for example, the lead in gasoline and paint, the radiation around nuclear power stations, the lack of any bans on night working or exposure to radiation for hospital nurses.[2]

Again, the choice for individual women who work in dangerous environments is a no-win one: to risk harm to oneself or her child, or to face exclusion.

Despite their prominence in the literature, women's biological dissimilarities from men normally make only a very small contribution to the sum total of ill-being at work. The main occupational hazards are socially, not biologically, constructed. They stem, not from bodily difference, but from gender-based power relations, from occupational segregation, and from women's role as caregivers.

These last two factors, in particular, are closely connected. Many of the positions women occupy in the workforce—cleaning, cooking, sewing, nursing, teaching, social work—are direct extensions of the work they do, unpaid, at home, and most are closely connected, directly or indirectly, with caregiving. A central component of caregiving, of course, is responsibility for the health and safety of others. If a child is scalded, the mother is blamed for not watching the saucepans; if her husband has a heart attack, it is because she failed in her duty to feed him only polyunsaturated fats; if her senile father-in-law wanders out of the front door and under a bus, it is her fault for not keeping a close enough eye on him.

From articles in women's magazines to posters in clinics the message is unvarying: it's the caregiver's fault. Rarely is it suggested, for instance, that the horrific toll of road accidents (in Britain, one child in five is, at some point, injured in a traffic accident) might have something to do with poor design of housing estates, or bad traffic planning, rather than individual parents' failure to teach their children the Green Cross Code. This attitude was exemplified by the Chief Medical Officer of Health for Aberdeen, in an interview in the *Guardian* on the subject of accidents in the home. Describing accidents as "the major epidemic of the twentieth century," he said that over half happened in the home, and that the most common cause was fatigue, since "most occur at the end of a period of maximum houshold activity or shortly after returning home from a strenuous day's work." So, what did he see as the best form of prevention? Perhaps housewives should get more chance to rest? Perhaps homes should be redesigned to make them safer? No, Dr. McQueen's solution was that "'the housewife must be taught to exercise special care when tired or worried, to remove potential causes of accidents and to overcome complacency." In other words, the woman's own well-being is a matter of supreme indifference; what matters is that the rest of the household should be protected from danger.

There can be few women, particularly among those who have spent time caring for small children, who have not internalized some of these attitudes. Not only do they routinely disregard their own well-being; they also feel guilty if anyone they are notionally responsible for is injured or becomes ill. And these attitudes, along with the caregiving roles, are carried across into the world of waged employment.

Hospitals provide one of the most dramatic examples. Here, women are concentrated in nursing, cleaning, catering, and clerical jobs, where their time is divided between caring for the patients and servicing the "profes-sional" medical staff, who are more likely to be male. Although hospitals are supposed to be places that restore health, for the people who work in them they are in fact extremely hazardous. Staff are expected to work exceptionally long hours under very stressful conditions. They are expected to lift weights that would be banned as too heavy in factories. And they are exposed to highly infectious diseases and toxic substances. Most nurses are daily expected to handle infected shit, vomit, blood, and urine and to run the risk of being scratched with infected needles or bitten by infected teeth. Many suffer from chronic fatigue, and serious back injuries are common. Yet taking time off to care for their own health is frowned on.

Similar tales could be told of nursery nurses, home aides, and care assistants who cheerfully sacrifice their own health to that of their charges. Here too this can be explained by reference to the family and the woman's role in it of protector of the health of the weak and dependent. What is less easy to explain is the way in which the ethos of self-sacrifice and disregard for one's own health also appears among women whose jobs do not, on the face of it, involve much caring at all—in factories, for example, or in offices or shops.

It seems the notion that one's own health doesn't matter is not job specific but part of the general condition of femininity. Although ostensibly the obverse of the macho notion that true masculinity involves risk taking (and that it is "feminine" to worry about dangers to one's health), conventional notions of what is feminine appear, ultimately, to produce the same result. While men don't complain about dangerous working conditions because it is "unmanly" to be vulnerable, women don't because it is "unfeminine" to be selfish. Thus are the hazards perpetuated.

Needless to say, not all women passively accept this role, and there have been numerous examples of groups of women workers who have been roused to militancy over health and safety issues. Nevertheless, the ideology of self-sacrifice (sometimes displaced as sacrifice to the cause of sisterhood or trade unionism) forms part of the context in which they must struggle.

The health effects of occupational segregation do not, of course, stop at their relegation of women to caregiving jobs. There is hardly an industry where there is not a sharp distinction between "men's" and "women's" jobs. In factories, women are concentrated in the most routine and repetitive assembly and packing jobs, especially those that involve "dexterity." In retailing, they operate cash registers and smilingly serve customers with low-value goods (while their male colleagues manage them and sell high-value, high-tech goods like cars, computers, or stereos). In offices, they occupy the lowest echelons of the career ladder, pounding keyboards, filing papers, and servicing the mainly male technical, professional, and executive staff. This segregation has several implications for health. At the simplest level, it means that women, being worse paid, are poorer than men. They are therefore—especially if they are lone caregivers or living alone—likely to be exposed to a whole range of stressors outside the workplace that may contribute to ill-being within it. They are more likely to be poorly housed, in polluted areas; they are less likely to be adequately fed; they are more likely to have to use inadequate public transport; they are less likely to have leisure, and so on. These stresses, added to the stresses of combining unpaid housework and caregiving with paid work, create a high "background level" of stress, which any additional stresses generated within the workplace may tip over into danger levels.

Unfortunately, in most of the occupational ghettos where women find themselves working, such additional stresses are there in abundance. Whether they are in factories, in offices, or in shops, the majority of these jobs involve the repetition of a narrow range of repetitive movements, often combined with intense visual concentration. In electronics factories, for instance, assemblers often have to squint down microscopes to see the tiny components they are working with; word processor or data-entry operators have to stare at a brightly lit screen while their fingers tap-dance across the keyboard. Additional stress is created by the pressure to work at speed. In some cases, workers are actually monitored by machines, which count such things as the number of keystrokes per hour, the number of customers dealt with, error rates, and how often they take a break. In other cases, the discipline is provided by payment systems based on results. The combination of holding some muscles in the body in rigid and unchanging postures while others are obliged to move repetitively as fast as they are able leads to serious and, in some cases, irreversible strain injuries.

Another characteristic of most of these jobs is that they are fixed to one spot, while men's jobs tend to be more mobile. Over the years, time-and-motion studies have demonstrated to employers the numbers of fractions of seconds that are wasted if assembly-line workers leave their posts to fetch a new batch of components, copytypists leave their workstations to retrieve something from a file, or checkout operators get up to replenish the stock of carrier bags. So all these excuses to stretch the limbs have been eliminated. If a machine needs servicing, this will normally be done by a man who roams freely about the building.

One would expect people who are immobilized in this way to be allocated more space than those who only touch base periodically during the course of a working day, but in fact the opposite is often the case. A stroll around most office blocks will reveal huge, empty, thickly carpeted rooms, containing enormous empty mahogany-and-leather desks and several capacious chairs for the use of single managers who may occupy them for only a few hours a week, while nearby, on vinyl floor tiles, rows of typists or data- entry clerks are crammed together all day with barely space to put down their handbags. Despite the high levels of static produced by the Visual Display Terminals (VDTs), their chairs and workstations will most likely be coated in synthetic materials, and their air-conditioning primitive.[3] Theirs will also be the area that looks out on the inner courtyard where the trash cans are kept, rather than the landscaped grounds or city skyscape framed by the managers' windows. The resulting cocktail of stresses (noise, poor ventilation, enforced exposure to the smoking or irritating habits of colleagues, poor temperature control, total lack of privacy, being physically constrained) produces a sense of ill-being that, despite the cheerful camaraderie of the oppressed, is almost tangible as one walks by.

However, the physical effects of confinement are not the only way in which such segregation produces ill-being. It is also experienced as an expression of the gender-based power system that operates in the workplace. These women, immobilized at their workstations, frequently in open-plan areas, are literally available to the men who walk freely through. If their work includes secretarial duties, their job descriptions place them at the service of certain specified managers for whom they work, but often it is assumed that in emergencies they can also be called on by other managers to carry out services not specified in any job description ("Just make us a cup of coffee, could you, love?"). Even men who are supposedly their equals or inferiors in rank (such as mail clerks or security guards) are free to interrupt and banter as they walk through.[4]

At its most benign, this permanent availability to male attention may be experienced as just a minor irritant or even as a source of pleasurable variety in an otherwise deadly routine. However, it can take the form of serious sexual harassment, making work a daily nightmare to be endured at the cost of health and well-being. Significantly, many of the worst cases reported of sexual harassment, where women have been systematically abused both physically and mentally by groups of men, have taken place when women have trespassed across the invisible frontiers between occupational categories and asserted their ability to do "male" jobs: on building sites, for instance, in the printing industry, or in the fire brigade. Here, the role of sexual harassment becomes visible, not as an enjoyable ingredient in the social life of the workplace that has got a little out of hand, but as the policing of occupational boundaries. Sexual harassers are like the Alsatian dogs patrolling the perimeter fences of high-security buildings, and most women, consciously or unconsciously, are aware that they may enter only by invitation, and then at their own risk. It is safer, by far, to stay well away.

I have tried to show in this chapter that the interplay between social factors and physical ones, both in causing ill-being at work and in the ways in which that ill-being is experienced, is exceptionally complex. In many cases, the social relations of the workplace have become embodied in the design of jobs, equipment, and buildings that carry with them specific physical hazards. The solutions will be equally multifaceted. It is not enough to find technical fixes or to redesign buildings or machines, although these may help. Neither is it enough to redesign jobs, although this too may eliminate some hazards. It is not even enough to attempt a radical reappraisal of the division of labor within whole industries, although this might bring changes that would benefit many women. To produce working environments in which women's well-being is safeguarded at all times, it will be necessary to transform the very social relations on which our society is based.

/ 7 / TELEWORK: PROJECTIONS

THIS CHAPTER EXPLORES THE DIFFERENT MEANINGS that have been assigned to the idea of the electronic homeworker over the past two decades and some of the assumptions that underlie them. While these assumptions tell us little about the likely future extent of telework, they give fascinating insights into the preoccupation and predicaments of the present.

It is one of life's ironies that few things reveal the stamp of their times more precisely, or date more quickly, than prophecies of what the future will be like. Look at pessimistic science fiction of the 1930s, for instance, with its megalithic Fascist/Stalinist architecture and endless assembly lines; or the fantasies of the 1950s where clean-cut nuclear families keep hold of their decent middle-class all-American morality in the midst of nuclear destruction; or larky 1960s space adventures where the women are all young and sport pastel-colored mini-tunics and white plastic boots, and the huge mainframe computers, with no visible source of energy, flash fairground colored lights and, after prolonged whirring of their giant tape decks, deliver any required fact in sepulchral speak-your-weight voices.

What these images reveal is not useful information about the future, but very culturally specific (and often spectacularly wrong) assumptions about what is universal and unchanging in human life, the direction of techno-logical progress, and the desirability of particular social developments. In other words, they do not tell us directly what is going to happen, but what their creators believe, hope, or fear will happen. To the extent that these creators are representative of others of their generation, this is, of course, useful information; people act on their beliefs and fears and hopes, and these actions, or reactions to them, will form the context that the next generation will map, react against, and extrapolate from, to form the basis of its own prophecies.

In this chapter, I would like to focus on one particular set of predictions that have reappeared at regular intervals for the last two decades, with a persistence which is rare in this rapidly changing field. It is my hope that an examination of the assumptions that underlie these predictions will shed light on what has actually been happening, and what the forecasters hope or fear will happen, and that this in turn will assist in the identification of the key interest groups whose actions or reactions will determine what happens next.

The predictions in question concern the use of information technology to enable people to work at a distance from their employers, generally at home. This development occupies so central a place in forecasts about the future of work that it is difficult to escape the suspicion that it has acquired a symbolic importance quite out of proportion to its actual prevalence.

The image that "teleworking" conjures up is a powerful one. To the plate-glass and steel city-center skyscraper it counterposes a rural cottage; to the bustling, humming life of a crowded office it counterposes domestic tranquillity; to the daily bodily crush on a rush-hour commuter train it counterposes a disembodied, abstract, almost ethereal form of communication that leaves the senses intact and unassaulted. Implicitly, it promises the best of both worlds: full participation in the international traffic of ideas and information and enclosure in the protective sanctuary of the home. The worker is safe, cocooned in familiar, womblike surroundings, yet linked umbilically to the great world outside. The veins and arteries of the maternal body are telecommunications networks, throbbing day and night with their sustaining flow of information. We seem to be offered a resolution of the age-old conflicts between the needs for adventure and for security, for communication and for privacy, for the excitement of the city and for the serenity of the countryside.

This is the stuff of which symbols are made, and it is my contention that the "electronic homeworker" has become a highly charged symbol, embodying for many people their hopes and fears about the future of work. However, the meanings it carries are not constant. Not only have they changed over time; they also vary according to how their holders are placed in relation to the technology, to their work, and to their homes: whether, for instance, they are men or women, employees or employers, living alone or caring for others, well or poorly housed, young or old, attracted to information technology, or repelled by it.

If these differing meanings are not unraveled, the image, for all its power, remains hard to grasp, knotted at the center of a confusing tangle of opposing attitudes. To change metaphors, we hear, so to speak, only a sort of static crackle, an emotional noise in which individual voices cannot be distinguished. Trying to extract some sense from this cacophony, as politicians do, the temptation is to divide them crudely into "yeses" and "noes," and this is what many commentators have done, analyzing attitudes toward telework almost exclusively in terms of two sharply polarized groups—optimists and pessimists, those in favor and those against, those who think it is good and those who think it is bad.

It is a curious fact, and further testimony to the power of the symbol, that few other aspects of work organization are discussed in this emotionally (and often also morally) charged way. Although they affect much larger numbers of people, you would never expect, for instance, to be asked in such all-embracing terms whether you were "for" or "against" part-time work, or overtime work, or assembly lines, or payment by results systems, or the use of migrant labor.

Because such crude polarization obscures more than it illuminates, I propose to try to avoid it in this chapter. However, like any other commentator, my views, however much they may strive for objectivity, are inevitably colored, both consciously and unconsciously, by my own particular situation and experiences and by the historic moment. It therefore seems only honest to begin with a brief account of the circumstances that may have influenced them.

I am, and have been for nearly a decade, a self-employed single parent, working from my home in a somewhat overcrowded inner London flat. My work is a mixture of research, writing, and lecturing and sometimes involves collaboration with others, either remotely or face-to-face. The room in which I work houses three computers, two telephones, a fax machine, two printers, five filing cabinets, six bookcases, and two desks. At the moment the room is also occupied by one co-worker. My income fluctuates alarmingly. I never go away for more than one night without taking the laptop. Since 1982 (when my daughter was born), I have carried out or been involved in the design or analysis of a number of surveys related to telework: a survey (I believe the first of its kind in Britain) of "high-tech" homeworkers; a comparative survey of "traditional" homeworkers; a survey of homeworkers and potential homeworkers with severe disabilities; a survey of mobile teleworkers; a survey of keyboard operators based in central pools for whom decentralization was being considered; large-scale surveys of workers' and employers' attitudes to remote work in four European countries; a comparative survey of teleworkers in fourteen German and British companies; a survey of "new forms of work" in five European countries; and exhaustive (not to say exhausting) reviews of the literature on telework at various times.[1]

So you could say that I am writing both as a practitioner of telework and as someone who is fairly familiar with what empirical evidence there is about it. However, this does not produce omniscience. On the contrary, because the two experiences are to some extent in tension with each other, it would perhaps be more accurate to say that it has generated a heightened consciousness of the complexities of the issues involved and a wary reluctance to overgeneralize. It should also be noted that, because most of my work has been based here, there is a British bias that will doubtless become evident in my choice of illustrative examples in this article.

Having declared my interests, let me return to the image of the electronic homeworker, which, although it had existed since at least 1957 in the literature about automation, made its first appearance in mass public consciousness in the early 1970s.[2] The context was the energy crisis—the sudden realization that the era of cheap and apparently limitless supplies of fossil-fuel-based energy was over. Home-based working presented itself first and foremost as a way of saving fuel, and was discussed in terms of the "telecommunications/transportation trade-off."

By the mid-1970s, researchers like Nilles and Harkness had produced detailed estimates of how many million barrels of oil would be saved per annum for each percent of the U.S. workforce working from home, and the word "telecommuter" had been coined.[3] According to this conception, the homeworker is simply someone who "telecommutes" (i.e., communicates by means of telecommunications) as a substitute for physically commuting to work. Other factors, such as the contractual relationship with the employer, the nature of the tasks carried out, and the location of the worker's residence, are assumed to remain constant, and the image of the sort of person this "telecommuter" is reflects that of the typical commuter. Popular imagery of the period almost invariably assumes this person to be male, working in a managerial or professional capacity, conforming to a corporate ethos and living in the outer suburbs.

Parallel with these ideas ran another, more general set, whose origins lay in the libertarian 1960s and could in some cases be traced back even further to the Beat Generation of the 1950s. These proposed more radical critiques of corporate industrial society, presenting information technology as a means of breaking down its vast inhuman corporations and greening its cities. Their catchphrases included "post-industrial society," "convivial technology," "the greening of America," and "small is beautiful," and they shared a generally optimistic vision of decentralized small workplaces, intercommunicating by means of advanced technologies.[4] They also shared a hippy-like hostility to bureaucracy and large-scale organizations, in which categories most would place oppositional organizations like trade unions as well as multinational corporations and government departments.

Perhaps in direct reflection of the authorship of the most influential books in this genre of popular futurology, the central character in this scenario of decentralized work is also implicitly male, though sharing more of the characteristics of the stereotypical "creative" worker than that of the "commuter." Compared with the telecommuter this remote worker is more individualistic and less conventional; more likely, one guesses, to be self-employed. Speculating further, we can imagine him in jeans, rather than a suit, and living in the country, instead of a suburb.

However, the two visions share many features in common: their central protagonists are both middle-class and male; they are both predicated on an assumption that the worker has freedom to choose where and whether to work (which in turn assumes a background of full employment); and they both assume the technology to be benign and capable of control by its individual users. By the end of the decade, these two visions had to some extent come together to form Alvin Toffler's notion of the "electronic cottage."[5]

In the meanwhile, however, rapid changes were taking place in popular attitudes to technology. By 1978, not only was it clear that the Western world was embarked on a period of major industrial restructuring, entailing widespread unemployment, but it was also clear that a central instrument of this restructuring would be information technology, popularly referred to as "the silicon chip." Suddenly, at least in Britain, the newspapers were full of headlines like "chips with everything" and television screens awash with series purporting to explain the "new industrial revolution" in tones that were a curious mixture of doom-laden prophecy and boyish excitement.

The doom-laden prophecy focused almost exclusively on unemployment ("Technology Could Put 5M Out of Work" predicted a typical *Guardian* headline in September 1978), while the boyish excitement, having been enthusiastic over the incredible cheapness and smallness of microprocessors compared with valves or transistors, tended to concentrate on the marvelous range of activities that could be carried out "from your own living room." A common device was to set up in the studio a "home of the future" in which the paterfamilias (sometimes accompanied by a deferential wife and children) sat, joystick in hand, before a screen in a comfortable living room, exclaiming in amazement as he found he could use a home computer to check his share prices, book a holiday, pay his bills, and investigate the latest cricket scores. It would also be possible, the viewer was told, for home banking, home shopping, and "even work" to be carried out in this way. The technology was presented essentially as an executive toy, and its users, once again, were assumed to be male and middle-class.

The consensus that had previously existed in the public mind about technology being basically benign was shattered in the face of these sharply contrasting views about its likely effects. While it was still considered Luddite in most circles to question the inevitability of technological progress, it was now legitimate to ask whether it was "a threat or a promise." At this stage of the debate, the possibility of being able to work from home was seen very much as part of the "promise" side of the equation; it had not yet come to seem a threat, but this situation was not to last long.

At about this time, cheap personal computers and word processors began to make their appearance in offices up and down the country on a noticeable scale. And the people who were expected to use them were not the male managers and professionals of earlier popular images but women in hitherto fairly secure, albeit menial secretarial and clerical jobs. A new imagery of computer use was in formation to accompany this change. Instead of being associated with white-coated technicians or senior executives, who were presented as "driving" or controlling them, computers began to be presented as instruments by which their passive female operators could themselves be controlled. Advertisements for word processors emphasized the silliness and unreliability (albeit combined with sexual attractiveness) of secretaries and emphasized the ways in which the technology could increase accuracy and productivity and make it easier for managers to monitor the clerical work-force. Much of the previous mystique, embodied in specialist programming jargon which had surrounded the computing process, was also stripped away. Computers were now so easy to use, it was implied, that even dumb blondes could learn how.

Initially, such ideas made no reference to home-based working. However they did begin to attract the attention of feminists, especially as this period coincided with a rapid increase in the unionization of white-collar women workers and the beginnings of an alternative analysis of the impact of information technology, based on working women's own experiences of computer-based work, which were sharply at variance with many of the media images. This analysis also drew on earlier critiques of industrial society, especially on the work of Braverman, whose notion of "deskilling" was adapted (not without some difficulty, given the historically close association of the category "skilled" with "men's" work in most industries) to explain the fragmentation, routinization, and increasing pressure of work that seemed to accompany the computerization of low-level white-collar work.[6] According-ing to this analysis, workers' only hope of protecting themselves from the exploitative and factory-like conditions produced by office automation lay in unionizing and bargaining collectively for more humane working condi-tions. Anything that separated workers from one another, therefore, was to be opposed. And homeworking, although it was still seen as a theoretical possibility rather than an immediate reality, came firmly into this category.

Feminist thinking on the subject was also informed by a prodigious literature, stretching back over two decades, on what was known in the 1950s and early 1960s as the "trapped housewife syndrome." Beginning with Friedan's analysis of the "problem which has no name," the isolation of women in the home had become central to feminist arguments about women's oppression, and many of the projects of the 1970s—from collective living arrangements to campaigns for nursery facilities—had been designed to break this down.[7] As the 1980s dawned, no explicit analysis of telework from a feminist perspective had yet been published, but there were many women for whom the prospect rang alarm bells.

The home was widely accepted as being the site not of leisure, as it was for men, but of oppression. In feminist literature it was the place where women were on twenty-four-hour duty working without wages to service their husbands, children, and sick or elderly relations, where they had no private space, and could, if married, be raped with impunity. Women who had no escape from it were likely to suffer from depression and loss of self-esteem and self-confidence. It was often compared to a prison.[8]

It was around the turn of the decade that an entirely new note was introduced into the public discourse on the effects of new technology; the notion that, as the then Labor, subsequently Social Democrat Member of Parliament Shirley Williams put it, "Microelectronics offers the opportunity of reuniting the family."[9] Although it echoed some of their concerns, this idea was not usually voiced by feminists. On the contrary, it was most often to be heard from people with an explicitly anti-feminist agenda: from Prime Minister Margaret Thatcher; from Kenneth Baker, at the time Minister for Information Technology; from bishops, and industrialists.

At first glance, the connection between the family and microelectronics is none too obvious. It is made unusually explicitly in a book by Mike Aldrich, managing director of ROCC Computers (formerly Rediffusion Computers) and closely associated with the British government's ill-fated cable policy, having been the main author of the influential report by the British government's Information Technology Advisory Panel (ITAP), *Cable Systems*, on which the policy was largely based. His book, complete with an introduction by Kenneth Baker, mainly consisted of plugs for his company's products—ROCC is one of the leading manufacturers of data-entry systems in Britian and was at the time investing heavily in viewdata (or videotex) systems, including home workstations—and it includes the following revealing passage:

No institution has suffered (as a result of industrial society) more than marriage. From an original Christian ethic of marriage "till death do us part" . . . to the 1981 UK statistic that 37% of marriages fail during the first five years, we can see the erosion of an institution that has been central to our civilization.

The growth of transient marriage and one-parent families is the counterpoint to the decline of the extended family and the gradual withering of family responsibility for the old, the sick, the handicapped, and the disabled. They have all become the responsibility of the State in the main because home-based family society could not cope.

If the underlying economic trends were anti-family in the past, perhaps the future offers better prospects for our basic unit of social organization because of trends in our working lives. In 1981, 60% of the total U.S. labor expense was consumed by office workers. The total size of this workforce dedicated to working with logical goods or paperwork continued to grow . . . . We have to face the fact that our society has changed from being blue collar to being white collar. This may change our attitude to work. It is not possible to deliver a steel mill to a cottage each day for the worker to use, but it is possible to deliver electronic paperwork to the cottage everyday. With the array of tele-communications products and services becoming available at ever-re-ducing costs in real terms, the burden of change must be toward home-centering our lives rather than town or city-centering as at present for work as we know it.

. . . The home is becoming more important, paradoxically, while the institution it shelters falters. Perhaps one of the reasons for marital instability is economics.[10]

Like so many other similar statements, this passage avoids mentioning the word *woman*. The family and clerical work are presented as abstract concepts, affecting everyone, rather than specific manifestations of women's work. Yet it is, of course, the changing role of women upon which the author is commenting. He laments the passing away of the days when women stayed at home caring for children, the old, and the sick and deplores their growing independence of men, expressed in economic activity outside the home and a resulting freedom to live and bring up their children on their own if they so choose. He also implicitly recognizes the need for women's work in the white-collar labor force. It is as a resolution to this apparent contradiction—society's simultaneous need for women's paid labor outside the home and their unpaid labor within it—that information technology is seized upon with such avidity: as homeworkers, women can do both at once.

The role of telework has been transformed. Instead of being a solution to the problem of commuting, or the problem of the cumbersome and alien nature of large bureaucracies, it has now become a solution to the problem of the breakdown of the family. With the change in role, the image of the teleworker has also been transformed. There has been a change both of sex and of status. No longer the male ex-commuter or autonomous artist, the teleworker is now a woman who, by implication "puts her family first," the corollary of which is that her work is relatively unimportant, something to be fitted in between emptying Granny's bedpan and washing the baby's diapers.

It was at about this time, too, that attention began to be paid to the actual experience of telework. It was discovered that the British software industry had, since the 1960s, been employing substantial numbers of home-based programmers, mostly women who had left office-based jobs in order to have children. Thanks in large part to the charismatic personality of its founder, Steve Shirley, and the assiduous efforts of its public relations officer, Rosemary Symonds, F International (later rechristened the FI Group), a software company entirely based on the labor of home-based women, was featured in innumerable press articles and radio and television programs in glowing terms.

Surveys based on interviews or self-completed questionnaires with individual homeworkers produced more ambivalent results. While a minority were successful entrepreneurs, most homeworkers worked for a single employer and suffered in some degree from isolation, insecurity, and low confidence and regarded their situations, though better than no work at all, as part of the price they paid for wanting to spend time with their families. Many, especially those who were treated as self-employed, were underpaid and lacked benefits they would have been entitled to had they worked on-site.[11] In fact, although most were middle class, they had some things in common with traditional homeworkers in manual occupations like sewing or packing.[12] For most of these women, telework did not present itself as a perfect solution to any problem; it was merely one of a range of possible compromises available to them during periods of their lives when they were torn between the irreconcilable demands of wage earning and child caring. The ambiguity at the heart of their situation rendered their experiences susceptible to a wide range of different interpretations.

Some, who feared that telework could become a means of destroying trade union organization, drew on it for evidence of exploitation, and there were calls from trade unions and other organizations representing office workers (such as the U.S.-based 9 to 5) for electronic home work to be controlled or even banned outright, as was argued with some force by the German trade union, IG Metall. Others, with equal fervor, argued that telework was a means of liberating women.[13]

Telework became established as a subject of controversy and, in the mid-1980s, was the focus of several weighty policy discussion documents and technology assessments, international studies, and conferences.[14] While the documents produced tended to analyze telework in a basically moralistic framework (attempting to find some acceptable central ground in a debate structured around arguments for/arguments against), yet another public discourse was developing, in which telework played a more instrumental role, and was discussed more dispassionately, as one of a range of possible forms of work organization.

The key word in this discussion was *flexibility*, and its subject was the restructuring of organizations to make them leaner and better able to respond quickly to market changes, particularly against Japanese competition. The new buzz phrases included "flexible specialization," "just-in-time production," and the "core-periphery model" of workplace organization.[15] Few of the ideas put forward in this debate were entirely new. The idea that automation could be used to individualize mass-produced products, for instance, had been advanced by Jones in his prefigurative series of articles on automation in *Design* in 1957–1958.[16] And diagrams explaining organizational structures by means of concentric circles had featured on overhead transparencies in management studies courses for at least two decades. What was new was that these ideas were not being advanced in an abstract way as an aid to general discussion about organizational forms but were being put forward prescriptively for immediate and concrete application.

Manufacturing companies that had survived the crises of profitability and great shakeouts of labor in the late 1970s and early 1980s were now reinvesting and looking for ways to expand without committing themselves to a large, permanent workforce. Some service industries, like retailing, were reorganizing, using automated point-of-sale technology to make themselves more sensitive to market changes, while others were seeking ways to reduce their fixed costs. Flexibility was presented as the means of achieving these goals. And flexibility was construed as flexibility for the employer: flexibility to change working hours, to switch workers from task to task, or to take staff on or drop them in response to demand. Managers were presented with a menu of options to choose from to bring about such flexibility: new shift patterns; annual hours contracts; multitasking agreements; temporary or fixed-term contracts; part-time work; subcontracting (in the public sector this was encouraged by means of privatization and compulsory competitive tendering); the increased use of part-time workers; and the use of home-workers. Telework was perceived simply as one of these options.

On the face of it, seen from this perspective the concept would appear to have been emptied of much of its emotional content and degendered. In fact, much of the literature on workplace flexibility refers, directly or obliquely, to women's needs for personal flexibility in the disposition of their hours to meet family needs, and elides these two quite different and generally incompatible needs to suggest that they are the same thing: that flexibility for the employer must also mean flexibility for the worker. There appears to be a general assumption that "core" workers are male and "peripheral" ones female, although there is surprisingly little evidence that this model is matched in reality.[17] In this scenario, then, teleworkers are still likely to be women, but this form of work is no longer being presented as a solution to the decline of the family; it is simply one available means of reducing an employer's overhead costs and increasing organizational adaptability.

Intersecting with this discussion is yet another, in which telework also makes a guest appearance: the debate on the enterprise economy. Here, telework is seen as an intermediary stage on the road to entrepreneurship. This idea was first publicized by Rank Xerox, whose "networking" scheme was launched in the early 1980s.[18] Under this scheme, senior executive and professional staff were given training in running their own businesses and set up as teleworkers with the guarantee of a minimum amount of work from Rank Xerox during their first year of independence.

Since then, some definitions of telework have included self-employed people working from a home base who happen to use computers during the course of their work. It is, in practice, impossible to draw a watertight line between small businesses operating from a home address and other forms of telework (or indeed satisfactorily to define any type of telework).[19] It is thus open to anyone who chooses to do so to perceive the growing population of self-employed people as a thriving pool of entrepreneurs, many of whom will go on to set up small businesses based outside their homes.

In this view, teleworkers have changed their image again. They are once more most likely to be male (almost all the Rank Xerox "networkers" were men), and they are not perceived as being tied down by domestic commitments but as being free agents, motivated to work long hours to establish themselves in a competitive open market. The problem to which they represent a solution is the "culture of dependency"; their function is to reinvigorate the economy, cut the welfare rolls, and inject new life into the traditional values of self-reliance and the free market.

I have touched in this chapter only on some of the more important problems to which telework is seen as a solution. There are, of course, others: the problem of the employment of people with disabilities, the problem of the economic regeneration of remote regions, the problem of providing a distraction-free environment for creative thought, to name just three. I hope I have shown that these "solutions" have engendered very different images of who or what a teleworker is, and whether telework is "'good" or "bad." It is impossible to conclude without asking the question, Which of these images conforms most closely to reality?

I am afraid that the conclusion I have come to may not be especially illuminating. It is this: telework is so nebulous and ill-defined a concept that it can hardly be said to exist in any clearly defined and quantifiable way; it exists more powerfully as an ideological construct than as reality; there is sufficient evidence to support virtually all of the differing and, on the face of it, often mutually incompatible ideas I have outlined above, but in no case is there enough evidence to indicate that any more than a minority of the workforce will be affected. There *are* people working from home with their employers' agreement in order to avoid commuting (but not all that many); there *are* individualistic types who find the large corporation so antipathetic an environment that they have set up "electronic cottages" for themselves (but not all that many); there *are* women working from home with computers because they cannot find satisfactory child-care arrangements who are entirely happy with the arrangement (but not all that many); there *are* others in similar situations who believe that they are exploited and underpaid (but not all that many); there *are* public and private sector organizations systematically investigating the transfer of some of their staff to home-based work (but not all that many); there *are* lots of people working from home who incidentally use computers in the course of their work, from plumbers to farmers to architects; and there *are* lots of people with jobs outside the home who sometimes use their home computers for an extra bit of work. To make things even more confusing, mobile phones and fax machines and laptop computers have made it possible for increasing amounts of work to be done on the move, making them no longer place-specific at all.[20] Because people do not live by information alone, the notion that a majority of the population could ever become teleworkers is far-fetched. However, all these categories are growing and seem likely to continue to do so.

To me, the most interesting feature of these different images of telework is not so much what they tell us quantitatively about what is happening, but the dynamics of their interactions with one another.

Let me end with one example drawn from an article by Tom Forester, "The Myth of the Electronic Cottage."[21] His theme, that telework is not likely to grow at the rate predicted in the 1970s, is hardly unusual. However, his manner of arriving at it is. He bases his argument almost exclusively on his own personal experiences, and those of a handful of friends, of working from home. True, he scans some of the literature on the subject, but in a fairly desultory way. For instance, a wide range of empirical and analytical studies that focus on gender issues are dismissed collectively as "raising specific issues of financial exploitation, conditions of employment, and the lack of trade union representation." His argument centers on the fact that for him "an initial honeymoon period of two to three years, which was accompanied by feelings of elation and high productivity, was followed by a less satisfactory period which was accompanied by feelings of loneliness, isolation, and a growing desire to escape 'the same four walls.'" Because his starting point was the essentially male notion of the "telecommuter" and its associated idea of the "electronic cottage," he was totally unprepared for an experience that any woman would recognize immediately as the "trapped housewife syndrome," and which a more careful reading of the feminist literature would have warned him about.

To extrapolate to the whole of humanity from one's own experience is, of course, highly dangerous. However, it is individual experiences like these, and the decisions they inform, that form the building blocks of social movements. We ignore them at our peril. For it is in the interplay between ideas and lived experience that new attitudes are forged, and these attitudes in turn form the basis of action. The extent to which the electronic cottage becomes a reality, and the specific forms that reality takes, will depend on the decisions taken by a range of social actors—large employers, entrepreneurs, creative individualists, women with dependents, planners. These decisions will not be monodirectional; nor will they necessarily be permanent. They will interact with one another to produce new and unexpected patterns; new areas of conflict will arise, and, in the resolution of these conflicts, new social forms will be negotiated. Whether telework will remain a useful term for describing some of these forms is anyone's guess. For the present, the concept is still up for grabs. Take it and enter your own meaning.

/ 8 / THE FADING OF THE COLLECTIVE DREAM: REFLECTIONS ON TWENTY YEARS OF RESEARCH ON WOMEN AND TECHNOLOGY

WHEN I WAS ASKED TO WRITE THE PAPER FROM WHICH this chapter is drawn, I found it extraordinarily difficult to find a focus for it. It seemed important to find something new to say about the relationship between information technology and women's employment, but every approach that occurred to me seemed, somehow, to involve a repetition of things I had already said, or written elsewhere. Even when new information could be added, or new texts referred to, it was difficult to identify new concepts. In short, the subject seemed to have gone stale for me. With a shock, I realized that it was nearly twenty years since I had begun grappling with these issues.

It then occurred to me that perhaps the most helpful contribution I could make to this discussion would not be to assemble, yet again, a selection of empirical evidence, nor to attempt, yet again, to develop an analytical perspective that might contribute to the construction of a conceptual framework for new research projects on technology and women's employment, nor yet to frame, yet again, a series of "demands" to protect or further women's interests in a technological society, worthy though any of these contributions might be. No, at the risk of seeming self-indulgent, it seemed that a more useful task might be to chart the history of the various projects in this area that I had been associated over the years, many of which could loosely be defined as feminist, to see what, if anything, could be learned from these experiences.

The purpose of doing this is not simply to place things on the record, or even to settle old scores, but to try to identify the concepts that have been used to make sense of the relationship between technology, women, and work, and how these have changed over the years. In some cases, this involves carrying out a sort of archaeology of the intellectual self, to unearth the theoretical assumptions we brought, consciously or unconsciously, to our debates and research hypotheses. Closely related to this project is a secondary aim of comparing and evaluating the research methodologies used in work on women and technology.

If there is such a thing as "feminist research" (which many doubt, including self-proclaimed feminists), it seems likely that its essential distinguishing feature is not so much a specific methodology or methodologies as an attitude, which can best be encapsulated in the well-worn but still potent proposition that "the personal is political." If feminism has done anything, it has surely put the subjective self at the center of the research agenda. On the one hand, it has insisted that the traditional objects of social research—the poor, the oppressed, women, children, the old, whoever they may be, should be listened to with respect, and granted their subjectivity, and that the researcher should validate their views of the world. On the other hand, it has focused attention on the subjectivity of the researcher, challenging the notion that the positivist ideal of detached objectivity is obtainable and insisting that the gender, race, and class of this person and the circumstances that have formed his or her intellectual development will color any piece of research. In television production there is a system called "chromakey" that is used when a foreground image (usually a person or an animal) is required to be seen against a different background. The effect is achieved by photographing the foreground image against a monochrome background (usually blue) and screening out the same color when filming the background scene. The two images can then be superimposed on each other without any apparent color distortion. In some ways, this system provides an appropriate metaphor for this view of research. In it, it is as though the researcher's taken-for-granted assumptions create a sort of color screen that renders whole areas of the spectrum invisible. The audience for this research, unless they are perspicacious enough to challenge these assumptions, will be required, so to speak, to look through a similar screen and will see an appearance of completeness. In the past it has often been women who have been rendered invisible in this way.

Although these notions have been adopted and refined by many researchers who call themselves feminists, post-1960s feminism cannot be credited with inventing them. The attempt to see the world through the eyes of the people who form the subject of the research has for decades been a common feature of ethnographic research. The political project of trying to build an alternative, oppositional ideology from the experiences of oppressed peoples can be traced back to the Maoist idea of "consciousness raising," and to Gramsci. Similarly, a rejection of the supposed objectivity of the scientist is common to many critiques of positivism that gained currency during the 1950s and 1960s. Nevertheless, it is probably true to say that these approaches to research have been developed and used more rigorously by feminists than by any other group over the past two and a half decades.

I am afraid that much of the work I have published on women and new technology over the past two decades has lacked such self-referentiality. This has been for several reasons. In the case of commissioned work, the terms of a client's brief have often dictated that the work conforms, in its methodology and presentation, with standard "professional" research practice. In other cases, work has been produced as a critique or as counterevidence to a dominant view published in weighty government or academic texts. Here, the need to be taken seriously has required the adoption of a similar pomposity of tone. In other cases, work has been produced as part of a collaborative project, often with a political objective, with a women's group, trade union, hazards group, or campaigning organization. Here, it has been necessary to submerge the individual identity of the authors in a collective "we" personifying the members of this group, or the people the group has been set up to represent.

However valid these reasons may be, I now believe that the work was in some ways flawed by this lack of self-reference. The need to appear objective and, indeed, even the need to win an argument can lead to oversimplification in the writing, and a suppression of some of the doubts, subtleties, contradictions, and hidden connections that can emerge from a more subjective account. It can also result in a tone that suggests the author has all the answers, and discourages readers from further speculation and from making connections with their own experiences.

In this chapter, I hope to redress some of these problems. It is thus a necessary part of this project that I write in the first person, and comment on my own personal experiences and relationship to the subjects I have researched. To do so, however, entails several dangers.

The first is the age-old danger, faced by every woman since Sappho who ventures into print, of being accused of immodesty or egotism.

The second, a little more difficult to live with, is the danger of being accused of poor scholarship or authorship. I have noticed that the sentence or paragraph that gets cut from one's manuscript by professional editors is invariably the one in which one uses the word "I." Although it may be dead in many respectable academic circles, positivism appears to be alive and kicking in the offices where academic journals and books are produced. Whether self-reference is regarded as unscientific, as anecdotal, or as simple showing off I am not sure, but I suspect that most editors have a strong internal model of what a "proper" conference paper, article, or scholarly monograph should be like and ruthlessly delete anything that does not fit it. Such processes are generally closely bound up with notions of professionalism. I can remember exercising similar forms of censorship myself when working as an editor twenty years ago.

As with editors, so with academics, even in oppositional fields like Women's Studies. The conventional structure of the academic text, with its grandiose opening placing the work in an overarching theoretical context, its "objective" presentation of the evidence, its tidy conclusion, its scrupulous citations, and carefully arranged bibliography, has little space for the untidy self of the author, which is normally smuggled in only in the form of references to previous publications or, occasionally, when reporting on the methodology of some sorts of social research, an oblique reference to ways in which some of the personal characteristics of the author might have affected interviews with respondents who did or did not share these characteristics.

The third danger is by far the most serious. This is that in chronicling pieces of work or social movements with which I have been involved I might appear to be taking full credit for them when in fact my role may have been relatively small. In a paper of this scope it is impossible to give full acknowledgment to all the people who have helped form these concepts, either directly or indirectly. In many cases it is no more possible to disentangle individual contributions from the collective effort than it is to identify which drops of water make up a wave. I hope that readers will understand that, in the pages which follow, when I write in the first person about any particular set of ideas I am not claiming ownership of them but am treating myself as an archaeologist treats a patch of soil, or a chemist a sample of material—as a test-bed whose component parts can be analyzed and sorted, in order to identify the answers to questions like: How did those ideas get there? Where have they come from? How have they changed? And how were they used? The answers to these, will, I hope, lead on to make it possible to address further questions: Are they still relevant? Can they be adapted to new situations in other times or places? Or are they as outmoded as the clothes we wore when we thought such things?

In this spirit, I should begin by describing the circumstances in which I first became involved in discussions about "new technology" (as it was then called) and work.

I was at the time (the early 1970s) working in the publishing industry producing books and audiovisual materials for schools. The industry was a notoriously low-paid one at the time, with poor working conditions. When I started, in 1970, a new graduate editorial recruit was paid an annual salary of £750 and received two weeks holiday a year, at a time when the average annual salary of a male non-manual worker was £1,862. Outraged by this apparent injustice, I became actively involved in attempts to unionize the industry. This entailed not only coming to grips with the structures of the National Union of Journalists, which represented editorial staff, but also of a plethora of other trade unions, still largely organized on a craft basis, representing secretarial staff, designers, warehouse workers, typesetters, and other specialist print workers.

Independently of this, influenced particularly by the writings of Sheila Rowbotham, I began to get involved with the emerging women's movement in Britain.[1] Many of the radicals I met in the National Union of Journalists had, like myself, been students during 1968, and brought with them into their union activities a set of beliefs that seemed rooted in the libertarian and/or Marxist student politics of the time. When these beliefs are examined in retrospect, several themes stand out as particularly important. One was a faith in the spontaneous ability of rank-and-file workers (once the causes of their oppression had been pointed out to them) to organize themselves, frame appropriate demands, and fight for their own liberation. This was associated with a mistrust of full-time union officials or other bureaucrats who, because their interests as a class were not the same as those of workers, would, if given a chance, always negotiate a "sell-out." A second theme was the importance of unity between different groups of workers. The pursuit of sectional interests by any particular group was seen as diversionary and divisive. Appeals to unity were often used to deter groups of women workers from pursuing demands for "special provisions" (such as maternity rights), which would, it was thought, alienate their male colleagues. The general atmosphere in which these themes were developed was one of heady political optimism. Despite the fact that the expansionary economic environment of the 1960s was already over, there was still a strong sense that things could only get better; indeed, in some circles it was defeatist even to mention the possibility that a socialist revolution might not be around the corner.

In this context, when the first rumors began to reach Britain of a new technology that would transform the nature of typesetters' work, the first response was to perceive it as a threat to workers' unity. Radical members of the journalists' union, together with a few colleagues from other print unions, decided that this issue could not safely be left in the hands of full-time officials and formed a worker-based group, led mainly by women, to research it. It was argued that if all the print unions did not stand firmly together, then journalists would be able to input copy directly, thus putting the typesetters out of work. This would weaken all the other unions, journalists included, because only the typesetters, traditionally very well paid, had the industrial muscle to bring the newspaper proprietors instantly to the negotiating table, a strength they had frequently exercised in the past by threatening or taking immediate strike action (of a type then known in the press as "wildcat strikes"), which could completely halt production of a newspaper.

The issues, then, were redundancies and trade union unity. Indeed, it was sometimes claimed that managers' sole reason for introducing new technology was to "smash the print unions." One member of the union working group visited the United States to find out what had happened when the technology was introduced there, and came back with information that reinforced this view. The possibility that VDT (Visual Display Terminal, also known as Video Display Unit) work might entail health hazards was mentioned in passing but not made much of. The fact that the skills required to operate the new technology were those of a typist—normally seen as a woman's occupation—was not the subject of comment, perhaps because journalism was at the time virtually the only occupation in Britain in which men were required to be able to type. In keeping with this analysis, the action enjoined on workers was resistance: they should boycott all new technology in the interests not only of preserving jobs but also of preserving union strength.

Although at the time I made no connection between the two discussions, while this debate was going on in the trade union I was reading every feminist publication I could find. Among the socialist feminists with whom I identified, two "demands" seemed to be the most important preconditions for women's liberation: economic independence and the socialization of housework. The former led to a focus on paid work; the latter to a focus on what was unpaid. I can remember spending a lot of time puzzling over the relationship between privatized, unpaid domestic labor and the money economy, helped by a large Marxist feminist literature (in which Jean Gardiner's name stands out as especially useful).[2]

In 1976 I got a job with a large company in the North of England, which owned a number of factories, as well as the publishing division for which I worked. It was a hierarchically organized establishment, with sharp contrasts between the conditions of the, mostly male, managers in the office and the, almost exclusively female, clerical staff. Such union organization as existed was dominated by men in managerial grades, and, together with one of these men who was sympathetic to feminism, I had already reached the conclusion that it would be necessary to hold women-only meetings if we were to find out what the real grievances of the majority of the workers were. It was here that I had my first direct encounter with the effects of new technology—in the ladies' room. One day I met a young woman there, sitting, doubled-up, with her head clutched in both hands, rocking backwards and forwards in what appeared to be considerable pain. When I asked her what the matter was she said it was "them machines," which gave her excruciating headaches. The machines turned out to be terminals connected to the company's mainframe computer, on which she was processing invoices. I decided to bring this up at the first women-only meeting we were organizing and included a reference to it in the publicity material produced for the meeting. At the meeting it emerged that, although currently only a minority of the clerical staff—mainly invoice clerks—was working on computer terminals, the company was about to introduce some mysterious new machines called word processors into the customer services department.

From their description I recognized that these machines bore some family resemblance to the "new technology" we had heard about in newspapers and realized that this technology was not just likely to affect the jobs of a few hundred male print workers but tens of thousands of female office workers. I started collecting all the information I could about them—attending office equipment trade fairs, reading the special supplements on microprocessor technology that were beginning to appear in the business press, and writing to the British Society of Social Responsibility in Science (which produced a magazine about occupational health called the *Hazards Bulletin*) to see whether anything was known about the health hazards of VDTs.

This last request elicited copies of two research papers on the subject, one American and one Swedish. By following up all the references in each, I was able to assemble a file of information on the subject. This contained some useful, albeit fairly technical, information on eyestrain and the ergonomics of keyboard work, together with some less informative articles dismissing 'radiation scares." To my surprise, I discovered that the possession of this file gave me the status of an "expert" on the subject. From other discussions with people involved in producing the *Hazards Bulletin* I gained a more general introduction to the ideas in general currency in the radical science movement at the time—that science is not neutral and that the general principle to be followed in any analysis of occupational hazards is that the design of the job, rather than the individual worker, is likely to be to blame, from which it follows that the solution to the problem is to redesign the job, rather than the worker.

In the meanwhile, I was getting involved with a group of people (academics, trade unionists, and community workers) who were setting up a resource and information center for trade union and community groups in the city. Influenced by new radical movements in community development and adult education, as well as the ideas of Paolo Freire, this was intended to provide a resource that would empower working-class people by giving them the information and resources they required to develop an alternative analysis of the forces shaping their lives and enable them to take action to change them.[3] The themes of spontaneous rank-and-file self-organization and of unity were still strong, but here there was also an admixture (derived from the community action tradition) of a recognition that in some circumstances people might require help (from what might be called professional community workers) to do this effectively. There were, however, fierce debates as to whether the role of the professional researcher should be restricted simply to researching and serving the information needs of these groups, or whether there was also a responsibility to offer political leadership.

At the point when we finally raised enough money to open this center, several things happened almost simultaneously. I left my job to work full-time at the center, the *Hazards Bulletin* asked me to write an article about VDT hazards, and the BBC produced a documentary about the employment effects of new technology, called *Now the Chips Are Down*, which dramatically increased public awareness of information technology. As a result of these combined events, in the week when the resource center opened we were inundated with letters and telephone calls from people who had read either the *Hazards* article or another (about the possible impact of new technology on office jobs in the area) in our Center's newsletter. These people were mostly office workers themselves or trade unionists in other industries where information technology might have an impact. They divided into two main groups: those who were already suffering from eyestrain or headaches from prolonged screen-based work and those who were worried that their jobs might disappear as a result of the introduction of information technology.

It was clear that if we were to be responsive to local demands for information, research on new technology would have to take a high priority in the work of the new center. It was at this point that I found a "new technology" label attached to myself and entered the public arena of debate about information technology. This took place in several different, if often overlapping, forums. At the radical end of the spectrum there was the Conference of Socialist Economists and the British Society for Social Responsibility in Science (both essentially study groups of socialist academics that also produced publications and organized conferences). However, during this period (1977–1980) there were also a large number of conferences on the subject organized by government and academic bodies and by employers' groups, trade unions, and professional organizations. Numerous television programs and educational films were commissioned and reports and popular booklets published. The issue was also taken up by women's groups for the first time.

On the academic Left, Harry Braverman was a dominant influence. His *Labor and Monopoly Capital* (1974) had launched a whole generation of labor process analysts, virtually all of whom (quite against the spirit in which Braverman had written his book) appeared to concentrate their attention almost exclusively on auto production workers.[4] Into the discussions on technology, which had previously focused on job loss and unity, was introduced a new subject, that of skill. It was generally assumed that the Fordist tendency of capital to introduce ever simpler industrial processes in order to deskill workers was an absolute one. New technology was simply an instrument of deskilling, so far as this school of thought was concerned. Jane Barker and Hazel Downing showed that it was possible to adapt Braverman's model so that it could be applied to the introduction of new technology into typing and secretarial work.[5] The idea that the concept of skill might be a problematic one when applied to women or that there might be situations when the introduction of a new process involving more difficult skills might be in an employer's interest were not receiving attention. When I wrote a paper that attempted to analyze the changing skill content of domestic labor using Braverman's notion of deskilling, it received a hostile reception from the men in the CSE Microelectronics Working Group.[6] As far as they were concerned, the automation of household tasks was unproblematically a "good thing" and did not require any further analysis. Because it was occurring in the "sphere of consumption" rather in that of production, it had no relevance whatsoever to their discussions.

There were also attempts to integrate an analysis of the effects of technological change into economic theory, both orthodox and Marxist. Kondratiev's idea of cyclical "waves" of technological development was much discussed. However, the specter of technologically induced mass unemployment remained the dominant theme. Although it was sometimes pointed out that this may be a transitional feature of a massive restructuring of capital, most commentators were at a loss when it came to understanding the basis on which the next boom would be launched. Robots don't buy cars, it was said, so where would the mass markets come from for the next wave of commodities to be produced? Again, there was enormous resistance among the male economists who dominated these debates to any suggestion that the automation of domestic labor might have anything to do with the generation of new commodities.[7]

Meanwhile, in the trade union movement, some firsthand experience of the introduction of the technology was beginning to accrue. The question to which most people wanted answers was: How many jobs will it destroy? In some circles any stance other than out-and-out opposition was still regarded as treachery. Sometimes negotiations on the conditions of introduction were refused, which was not in the interests of the workers (generally women) who ended up having to use the machines. In other cases, the white-collar trade union representatives responsible for representing workers' interests in the negotiations were drawn from precisely those strata of lower management, professional, and technical staff who had the most to benefit from the new technology. They were perceived as the cause of, rather than the solution to, the problem by the secretarial and clerical women workers who had most to lose. In some cases this led to increased militancy among the women workers, many of whom, for the first time, put themselves forward for elected union positions and eagerly attended conferences on women and new technology organized by women's groups or trade unions. The technology-related issues they were most concerned with were health and safety, job design, and access to training. However, it was clear that in many cases these were inseparable from the other problems they faced as women in their workplaces. Meetings called to discuss technology often ended up discussing how to deal with the sexist attitudes of male trade union colleagues or the opposition of husbands or lovers to women being active in the union at all. I can remember one woman (a convenor in a factory that manufactured cosmetics) whose husband would wait impatiently outside the meeting room for her to finish, looking angrily at his watch and accosting anyone else who came out. Another (a school secretary) had been told by her husband to choose between him and the union ("Well," she told me, "I thought about it for a while and then I decided, I'll take the union, thank you very much!").

In the literature we produced at the time there is usually a silence surrounding these problems. Much was written about the burdens of the "double shift"—the combination of paid work and unpaid housework. Little, however, was said in public about the third shift—the work for the union. In retrospect, this was often more burdensome and brought fewer rewards than either of the others. At its worst, it involved spending exhausting hours in drafty, smoky meeting rooms, in the company of abusive, argumentative men (many of whom would have been completely at a loss socially without a meeting to go to), getting home to an uncleaned house and an empty refrigerator long after the shops had closed, being attacked as a militant by the Right and a reactionary by the Left, never thanked, always blamed, while relationships fell apart about one's ears. As the 1970s progressed, the euphoric moments of victory became ever rarer.

Yet the tone of our publications was relentlessly optimistic. Between 1976 and 1980 I was working on the manuscript of an ambitious *Working Women's Handbook,* supposed to be published by Pluto Press in their Workers' Handbook series. Delayed by overwork, illnesses, and bereavements in my own life and overtaken by events (the Thatcher government, once elected in 1979, immediately began to dismantle much of the legislation I had so painstakingly anatomized), this book was never quite finished and remains unpublished to this day. Its language and approach are, however, typical of the period. Each section starts with an analysis of a problem (for instance, lack of child-care facilities or low pay), illustrated by tightly edited quotations either taken directly from working women I had interviewed or gleaned from secondary sources. The tone then shifts to a more prescriptive one ("This is what you can do about it"), again copiously illustrated with examples of how particular groups of women workers have successfully overcome it. The collection of all this information, in which I was greatly helped by Jo Fitzpatrick and Marianne Dee, involved not only following up large numbers of personal leads, through contacts made at meetings or conferences, but also the accumulation of large files of newspaper cuttings, magazine articles, pamphlets, and books. It could not have been achieved had we not been simultaneously setting up a library of such information at the resource center. What strikes me when rereading this material now is the curious shift in emotional tone from the extreme pessimism of the way in which "problems" are presented to the inspirational triumphalism of the "solutions." The combined effects of capitalism and patriarchy are presented as producing such an enormity of suffering that language can hardly contain it, yet in these accounts women organizing together, fueled by feminist understanding and righteous anger, generate such a glow of sisterhood, such strength, that they appear to become invincible. I do not think that this was mere projection or wishful thinking. It is so general in the socialist feminist literature (and in some films) of the time that I am convinced it expresses something we really felt, an emotional atmosphere we breathed, then, but is difficult to describe now without resorting to clichés.

Trade unions were not, of course, the only arena in which women were active then. There was a proliferation of small single-issue groups many of which, by the end of the 1970s, had begun to address various aspects of the relationship between technology and women's lives. Some, either seeing the technology as inevitable, or as "neutral" and desirable, saw women's exclusion from science and technology as a major problem, and began to agitate for more training for women and, where necessary, for that training to be carried out in women-only groups. Feminist teachers set up projects in schools and colleges, while other women set up groups to raise funds for women's technology training centers. One of the first of these, if not the very first, was the East Leeds Women's Workshop, in which Lynette Willoughby, a feminist electronics engineer, played a key role. There was some debate as to what the purpose of such training was. Were women to be trained simply to fill low-level niches in a system that exploited them? Were

a favored few to be given access to "male" skills so that they could climb a
"career ladder" leaving most of their sisters behind? Were women to be
educated *about* the technology rather than *in* it, so that they could develop
a critique of an essentially male technology? Or was the technology neutral,
capable of delivering good things to society if only it were controlled by
women with humanitarian motives, rather than by men with destructive
and profit-seeking ones? After a decade in which women have been urged
to become assertive, independent, and autonomous (not to say greedy) such
questions now have a curiously old-fashioned ring to them.

Concern about the neutrality and control of science and technology
were not exclusive to the discussion of information technology. These
debates were paralleled and cross-nourished during this period by lively (and
in some respects more advanced) discussions among feminists about medical technology and its impact on women's lives, and the beginnings of a
public debate about the relationship between gender and military technology (which was to culminate several years later in the Greenham Common
peace camp).

Another important set of concerns was the role of transnational corporations and the development of international solidarity between women.
Copies of Rachel Grossman's (1979) description of conditions in the silicon
chip factories of Southeast Asia had reached the United Kingdom by 1979,
and profoundly shocked many women who had focused their attention on
the impact of information technology on the work processes of the user
industries, forgetting to ask how it was itself produced.[8]

In 1979 and 1980, several feminist conferences on women and information technology were held, each well-attended. I still have the stencilled
double-sided sheet of paper that was handed out—before photocopying was
easily available—to advertise one of them, organized in the name of the
Yorkshire and Humberside Regional Socialist Feminist Group. This conference gave birth to the West Yorkshire Women and New Technology Group,
which later produced a special issue of the magazine *Scarlet Women* on the
subject in 1982. The leaflet still seems to me one of the best summaries of
"Why New Technology Specially Affects Women" (the title of the paper)
while still giving off a pungent odor of its time. The rhetorical question of
the title was answered under four main headings: "Because of the sorts of

jobs we have"; "Because we also work at home"; "Because of how we are educated"; and "Because economic crisis hits women hardest." Under these four headings it manages to work in a remarkably complete agenda of the issues that were of major concern at the time. Those included: "skill loss"; "double shift"; "mobility"; "trade unions"; "consumption"; "homeworking"; "unemployment"; "cuts"; and "multinationals." After an anxiety-provoking run-through of all the detrimental effects on women's lives the new technology was likely to bring, the leaflet ends with a series of open-ended questions, under the general heading: "Could new technology bring women's liberation?" I can remember writing it, with Jude Stoddart, after an exhausted brainstorming session, late one night, typing straight onto a Gestetner stencil with a mechanical typewriter. The need to say everything on two sides of A4 paper, to keep the language simple, and to avoid saying anything that might lead to an inadvertent interpretation that was not politically correct, meant that every word had to be carefully scrutinized before it was committed to the stencil. Not much room for subjectivity there.

In 1979 the center where I worked actually received some money (from the Equal Opportunities Commission) for research on the impact of new technology on women's working lives. This meant that, for the first time, I had to grapple with some serious methodological problems. There did not appear to be a single academic discipline that could provide the tools for any systematic analysis of the social impact of technological change. During the 1960s, as a summer job while a student, I had worked as a reporter on a series of interdisciplinary conferences on the "City of the Future" and had picked up a little knowledge of forecasting techniques, but even futurology seemed to be of little help here. The relevant books I could find were scattered across library shelves: some in economics; some in sociology; some in psychology; some in medicine; some in technology; some in geography; some in "business studies"; some in the newly emerging "women's studies" and "trade union studies" sections. Many of the most useful pieces of empirical information came from none of these, but from trade journals, newspapers, conference papers, and government reports. Yet these often had a certain circularity. A tentative speculation made in one quarter would be published as a prediction in another, which would then be cited as an authoritative source in a third. The unique library classification system we had at the resource center (devised by Marianne Dee) meant that these could all be filed together under commonsense headings related to the research in hand, and made it possible to develop some sort of overview of the literature (a resource frequently used, usually without acknowledgment, by visiting academics). Nevertheless, this did not necessarily produce a very coherent conceptual framework. I found myself collecting scraps of empirical information, almost randomly, and then sorting them and re-sorting them until I could identify headings under which they could be grouped without too much distortion.

A central difficulty was finding quantitative information that would enable me to assess the relative importance of different types of women's employment. Which sorts of jobs were likely to be automated? And how many women were employed in such jobs? All the up-to-date employment figures I could find were based on industries, rather than occupations. Research done in the past on the distribution of occupations within industries was useless for my purposes because it aggregated the figures for men and women, making gender segregation invisible.[9] In order to collect this information and establish the long-term trends in occupational change and changes in their gender composition, it was necessary to go back to the primary sources (censuses of population and employment, going back to the beginning of the century) and spend many tedious hours with a calculator (a task I could not have achieved without the unstinting help of Quentin Outram). This was my first firsthand encounter with official statistics, and it was a very disillusioning one.

I was aware of the work of the Radical Statistics Group, which was about to publish a book called *Demystifying Social Statistics*, so I was prepared to find that the statistics embodied values that might be regarded as "establishment" ones.[10] However, up to that point I had somewhat naively believed in the comprehensiveness of official data. It came as a great shock to me to discover that, on a range of issues which one might have thought would have been important to the government for its own policy-making purposes, the relevant statistics just did not exist. It would be several years before I became confident enough to formulate specific criticisms of government research-gathering instruments, or suggest changes to them. At the time, I simply felt lost and lonely, stranded without a map in a jungle of conflicting facts. This existential angst is, perhaps, an inescapable part of the process of becoming a researcher. As the certainties crumble and hypotheses collapse, we discover that there is no parental god up there with the "right" answers, and it is up to us to construct our own version of reality. I cannot say that I am used to it yet. I still write with the expectation that somewhere a reader will be taking each sentence apart, pointing out factual errors or logical flaws in the argument, and I am not sure whether I am relieved or disappointed when, having sent the finished work out into the world, there is no reaction at all, apart from citations in other people's, equally anxious, productions.

This is not the place to describe this research in detail. It did, however, establish a pattern in my life which was to last for nearly a decade, whereby each piece of research was essentially written up twice: once in the accepted scholarly way, for the client who had funded it, and then again in a popular form, for "ordinary people." As the 1980s progressed, this became more and more difficult to do as the organizations that were willing or able to publish the popular versions dwindled in size and number. In the absence of successful mass movements or any large-scale public culture of resistance, it also became more difficult to identify who this "ordinary person" might be for whom one was producing these materials. Nowadays, having lost any sense that I have the "right answers," I am increasingly uncomfortable using any authorial voice that is not identifiably my own. But this is a digression. In 1980, despite the unmistakable signs of an impending recession and the most reactionary and anti-woman government in living memory, it still seemed vitally important to make everything one learned available, as quickly as possible (while it was still warm, so to speak), to the widest possible working-class audience. I wrote *Your Job in the Eighties* (intended as a popular women's guide to the effects of new technology on employment) in a two-week burst (fueled by the high blood pressure of mid-pregnancy) in 1981, but its spirit is from the 1970s. It still has the "you too can do it; all you need is organization and courage" tone of the rallying publications of the previous decade. It focused exclusively on collective action, implicitly suggesting that the individual, acting only as an individual, is powerless.[11]

During the early 1980s this mood was to change. The individual members of the discussion and campaigning groups of the later 1970s went their separate ways. Some went to work for the Greater London Council or one of the other newly radical local authorities that seemed, for a time, to offer the possibility of islands of socialism within the greater sea of Thatcherism. Some became academics. Some withdrew into child-bearing and domesticity. Some went to work full-time for trade unions, charities, or campaigning bodies. Some set up training projects or consultancies or other new enterprises. Some retrained so that they could practice psychotherapy or osteopathy or other more esoteric alternative therapies. Some became professional politicians. Some died. As survival became more difficult and the experience of political defeat more common, only a few, with exceptional stamina, managed to sustain the rhythm of regular meetings and continue to engage in discussion for discussion's sake. Activities that had previously been carried out in people's spare time, for their own sake, without payment, were increasingly becoming the preserve of a professionalized "'voluntary sector." It was often difficult to tell whether people were speaking from their own political beliefs or regurgitating the terms of their job descriptions.

These changes inevitably led to a shift of focus, often a narrowing of it, more directed to the achievement of realizable short-term goals: the setting up of a particular training course; the opening of a women's center; a change in policy. A new and pragmatic generation was emerging, familiar with feminist and socialist ideas because they had heard them from radical teachers at school and university, but also hard-nosed about their own survival. They often made the veterans of the 1960s feel hopelessly naive and unrealistic. Many of the theoretical debates of the 1970s were left unresolved because they suddenly seemed irrelevant. The contents of the shelves of feminist book shops changed out of all recognition. When I looked, in about 1984, under the heading "employment" in *Sisterwrite* (my local feminist book shop) expecting to find, as I would have a decade earlier, a selection of heavy works of political economy, campaigning pamphlets, autobiographical accounts, and sociological studies, all I could find was one book about sexual harassment at work, three guides to setting up one's own business, and a large number of handbooks for developing greater assertiveness. It wasn't that feminist publishing had declined. Far from it. There were shelves and shelves of poetry and fiction, books about sexuality, about race, about health, about housing, about violence, about psychology. It was just that the attention had shifted away from those previously central concerns of economic independence and the study of work, whether paid or unpaid. I tried looking under "technology" and found a few collections of essays about women's relationship with technology, but these were heavily outnumbered by "how to" books about computing. What seemed to have happened was a radical shift of emphasis from the collective to the individual.

This change did not happen all at once, however. During the early 1980s an immense amount of empirical work was done on employment, technology, and gender, often designed to test the hypotheses we had developed in our discussions in the late 1970s. Ann Game and Rosemary Pringle, in Australia, published *Gender at Work*; Cynthia Cockburn in Britain published *Brothers*.[12] It became clear that skill was a much more complex concept than Braverman had supposed, more a social construct than any acquired set of competencies that could be objectively measured for their difficulty. It also became clear that the impact of information technology on women's jobs was far more diverse than simplistic Marxist analyses had predicted. It was true that in some industries and some occupations there was a Fordist tendency to reduce tasks to their simplest components, minimizing the skill requirements and reducing the workforce to a homogeneous, interchangeable mass. In others, however, the introduction of new technology obliged workers to acquire a lot of new skills. Because they were usually fairly low-paid women, and the technology was seen by their employers as an extension of the typewriter, clerical workers were often not provided with adequate training. The word "re-skilling" began to be used alongside "deskilling," and evening classes in word processing had long waiting lists.

Many of us were still grappling with broader theoretical and political issues, trying to tease out the implications of what we had learned and apply them to other debates. I can remember, for instance, writing an article in which I attempted to apply Marx's theory of alienation to domestic labor, by developing an analogy between the worker's relationship with the means of production in the workplace and the housewife's relationship with the means of reproduction (the home itself and domestic technology). Because workers were increasingly being required to become owners of these means of reproduction, I argued, they could not express their hatred of them and organize against them as factory workers could, although they were just as surely enslaved to the cash economy by the need to pay for them. I wanted to develop this argument to explore questions of what sorts of self-hatred and neurosis might ensue from this relationship, but lacked the courage to do so. I had so often been put down by academic Marxists for arguing "on the wrong level of abstraction" that I dared not risk it again. Instead, I swung back to a discussion of high-tech homeworking, the subject on which I had originally been asked to write.[13]

Meanwhile Rosemary Crompton was carrying out research (published under the title *White-Collar Proletariat)* that brought detailed empirical evidence to the debate about how the working class is to be defined, challenging Marxist orthodoxies in the process.[14]

An idea that received a good deal of attention during this period in discussions of technological change was that of "socially useful production." The charismatic figure of Mike Cooley, who had been the main architect of the Lucas Aerospace workers' "alternative plan for Lucas" was largely responsible for this.[15]

When asked to produce a feminist critique of this idea, I found myself returning, yet again, to the subject of domestic labor and its relationship with the money economy. It was, I thought, the emphasis on commodity production (and with it, the idea of the "'real worker" as somebody exclusively engaged in commodity production) that was suspect in any vision of alternative work that was supposed to prefigure a socialist society. Was the socialist dislike of service sector employment simply a consequence of its being largely identified with women's work, or were there more complex issues at stake? I realized that the relationship between unpaid labor, service employment, and commodity production was a dynamic one, whose boundaries were constantly changing, partly in association with the introduction of new technologies. The history of capitalism could be seen as the history of the gradual drawing into the money economy activities that had previously been carried out unpaid in the household. An essential part of this process was that of commodification, and each wave of new technology generated new commodities. The introduction of these commodities brought changes in work processes (and hence in skills) both for the workers involved in their production and for the users of these commodities. To attempt to freeze a particular set of skills or work processes and apply them to the development of "alternative" commodities seemed likely to be doomed to failure. Even if it succeeded, it would most likely be anti-woman in its effects, since it would also freeze the particular form of the division of labor (and hence of social relations) of the moment in which it was captured.[16] Increasingly, however, such articles seemed to produce no response. One might as well have dropped them into a void for all the debate they generated.

By 1982 I was living in London, alone with a baby, carrying out research on what later came to be known as "teleworking" (a clumsy attempt on my part to translate the French coinage *teletravail,* used to refer to work carried out at a distance using information technology). This relative isolation may have colored my experiences of the next few years. It was certainly the case that I felt distanced from whatever political debates were going on. Instead of being carried out voluntarily, the research going on in the areas I was interested in was increasingly being funded in academic, local government, or voluntary sector contexts. A note of wariness and competitiveness began to creep into the discussions when researchers met one another. Although for some, knowledge was still something to be shared as widely as possible, so that common learning could take place, for others it was clearly a valuable commodity, to be parted with only for money, promotion, or glory. There were still some occasions, like the conferences organized by the Women and Computing Network, that retained the atmosphere of the 1970s, but other, more academic ones seemed imbued with a more guarded and self-seeking atmosphere. There was a terrible conflict between the sharing feminist ethic and the need to earn a living. Because I was now self-employed, survival was hard, and I sometimes felt exploited when my work was used by others without acknowledgment or payment. However, I also felt a great need to be part of an intellectual community where ideas could be freely shared, and realized that I could not have it both ways. It was my impression that, in Britain at least, such a community hardly existed anymore, although on the rare occasions when I could afford to go to conferences in other countries, my faith in the possibility of its existence was rekindled.

The first such occasion was a conference on women and new technology organized by ISIS in Switzerland in 1983. There was a sense of excitement and urgency to communicate, which made one realize how demoralized feminists had become in Britain under the Thatcher government. There was a wonderful paper from a group of women from the Japanese Committee for the Protection of Women in the Computer World.[17] Trini Leung, from Hong Kong, spoke movingly and inspiringly about the need for international solidarity among women working for multinational corporations in the electronics industry, and there were thought-provoking contributions from many other countries. I came away convinced that continuing to bang one's head against the brick wall of Thatcherism, as so much of the British Left was doing, was not the best strategy. Instead, we should be concentrating on developing international links and confronting international capital.

The work I had been doing on teleworking had made me aware that when new technology is introduced it can facilitate changes not just in the nature, but also the location, of work. This does not just involve shifts from the office to the home or from the city center to the suburb, but may involve regional or international shifts. It seemed possible that the sort of international division of labor that had grown up in manufacturing industries during the 1960s and 1970s might well be repeated in service industries in the 1980s and 1990s. Helped by some leads from Judith Gregory at the U.S. office workers' organization 9 to 5, I had begun to collect information about the growing use of offshore information processing by companies based in North America, Europe, and Australia. I was not able to find funding to develop this work systematically, but it undoubtedly informed the work I was doing with women's groups at the time, most notably in the setting up of the City Center, a resource center for office workers in the City of London (in which Sarah Stewart played a key role) and in Women Working Worldwide, a group specifically set up to develop international solidarity among working women, into whose development Gerry Reardon and Helen O'Connell put an especially impressive amount of energy. In general, there appeared to be something of a retreat from internationalism in the British Left at the time, although there were some exceptions. The Greater London Council sponsored some work on multinational corporations (notably Kodak and Ford) and funded the London Transnationals

Information Center, but such initiatives often seemed to be regarded as aspects of development education, as do-gooding, rather than real politics. As the 1980s ground on, either feminist initiatives on new technology became scarcer or I lost touch with them. Such projects as there were seemed mainly addressed to practical issues. The Women and Computing Network gave birth to Microsyster, a project set up to provide training and computing services to women's groups, as well as a lively newsletter. Otherwise, my main contact with the issues was through correspondence with Ph.D. students, visits from overseas researchers, and the occasional conference. Much of my paid work did not relate directly to technology, although there was a steady trickle of interest in teleworking. I have written elsewhere at length about the different meanings this concept acquired.[18]

It is, though, perhaps worth noting two central preoccupations in relation to technology that surfaced during this period, which had been largely absent during the 1970s. The first of these was the concern, already referred to, with the spatial dimensions of technological change. Here, I found relatively little that was useful in either feminist theory or Marxism. The most creative thinking in the area seemed to be going on among radical geographers, such as the researchers at the Center for Urban and Regional Development Studies in Newcastle and in some work on racism and imperialism, notably that of A. Sivanandan at the Institute of Race Relations.[19]

The other concern was with the ways in which information technology not only changed the labor process itself but was associated with transformations in relationships between employers and employees, in particular its role in bringing about the casualization of employment. When I had discussed the possibility of writing a book on the subject of the casualization of employment with Pluto Press in 1982, I was told by the editor concerned that there was no such word, and that even if we were to coin it, the concept would have no meaning for people. Over the ensuing decade it became abundantly clear that even if the word was not known, the condition was being experienced widely. Under the rubric of "flexibility," large numbers of previously secure, permanent jobs were becoming temporary or casual, or farmed out to subcontractors and agencies, helped in no small measure by government policies that removed employment protection from large sections of the workforce, dismantled minimum wages, and obliged public employers to subcontract many of their services. In the discussions about casualization, however, the role of technology became less and less important. It was clear that though it was often a facilitator of casualization, the technology did not itself cause these social and legal changes.[20]

Perhaps partly because during the 1980s most of us had ourselves become direct users of information technology (I acquired my first personal computer in 1983, a modem in 1985, a fax in 1987), it was becoming harder and harder to focus on it as a separate issue in its own right, and the earnest debates of the 1970s about whether or not it was a "good thing" seemed at best irrelevant, at worst downright silly. For most people in Britain under the age of forty, information technology was now a taken-for-granted feature of everyday life. It had become necessary to be familiar with it or risk being seriously disadvantaged in one's career. Ten years after I had written that first *Hazards Bulletin* article about VDT hazards, I suffered the supreme irony of developing repetitive strain injury while working on a book on that very subject, commissioned by the London Hazards Center.[21] Since then, I have discovered that many of my women friends who are writers have developed the same condition.

This brings me to what is, perhaps, the central paradox of so many feminists' lives—our failure to practice what we preach. We write about the dangers of stress-related illnesses while leading incredibly stressful lives ourselves. We fight for the rights of low-paid workers while often accepting pitifully low fees or working for nothing ourselves. Some of us write about the exploitation and isolation of casually paid homeworkers, while working as home-based freelancers ourselves. We encourage other women to act collectively out of self-interest and not allow themselves to be guilt-tripped into self-sacrifice while we ourselves take on the most self -punishing roles in the interests of the common good. Are all our goals mere projections of our own unexpressed needs? In puzzling over such questions I find myself returning again and again to the conflict between individualism and collectivism. In retrospect, it now seems to me that of all the changes that have taken place over the last two decades, perhaps the most important has been the erosion of any belief in the power of collective action, and the slow dawning in each of us of the depressing realization that if we don't do it for ourselves, the chances are that nobody else will do it for us.

It seems to me that this has not just led to demoralization among people with a political commitment to try to make life better for working women; it has also led many thousands of individual working people to make choices in their lives (which they might not have made in less fearful times) that, together, have transformed the nature of employment and other features of their working lives. Losing faith in the possibility of public organizations being able to remain good landlords, they have bought their previously rented apartments. Losing faith in the possibility of getting their children decently cared for in public child-care facilities, they have chosen to work from home and look after them themselves. Losing faith in the possibility that their trade unions can secure their future, they have chosen instead to put money into private pension schemes. The sum of all these individual decisions has been a near complete collapse of the public infrastructure in which new collectivities can be woven. I do not know whether this British experience has been reflected elsewhere in the world, although the news stories from Eastern Europe suggest that features of it are certainly evident there.

What does seem apparent to me is that any solutions we might wish to propose, any demands we might wish to make for the future, must take this context into account. It may be that there is still the possibility of generating some enormous, collective act of hope that will enable people to begin trusting each other again. Failing this, we must try to find demands that do not force them to make a harsh choice between self (and individual certainty) and others (and possible loss). We cannot demand altruism. The best we can do is to trust people to see where their own best interests lie, and pursue them, with or without the aid of information technology.

/ 9 / MATERIAL WORLD: THE MYTH OF THE WEIGHTLESS ECONOMY

"THE DEATH OF DISTANCE," "WEIGHTLESS WORLD," the "connected economy," the "digital economy," the "knowledge-based Economy," the "Virtual Organization."[1] All these phrases were culled from the titles of books published in the six months prior to writing this essay, in spring 1998. They could have been multiplied many times: "virtual," "cyber," "tele-," "networked," or even just "e-" can, it seems, be prefixed interchangeably to an almost infinite range of abstract nouns. Without even straying from the field of economics, you can try "enterprise," "work," "banking," "trade," "commerce," or "business" (although the device works equally well in other areas; for instance, "culture," "politics," "sex," "democracy," "relationship," "drama," "community," "art," "society," "shopping," or "crime").

A consensus seems to be emerging—in economics as in other fields— that something entirely new is happening: the world as we know it is becoming quite dematerialized (or, as Marx put it, "all that is solid melts into air") and that this somehow throws into question all the conceptual models that have been developed to make sense of the old material world. We are offered a paradoxical universe: geography without distance, history without time, value without weight, transactions without cash. This is an economics that sits comfortably in a Baudrillardian philosophical framework, in which all reality has become a simulacrum, and human agency, to the extent that it can be said to exist at all, is reduced to the manipulation of abstractions. But these books have not been designed as contributions to postmodernist cultural theory, far from it. Frances Cairncrosss *Death of Distance* comes with a glowing testimonial from Rupert Murdoch on the front of its shiny blue dust jacket, and Diane Coyles *Weightless World,* not to be outdone, carries an endorsement from Mervyn King, executive director of the Bank of England, on its back cover. These are not academic inquiries into the nature of the universe; they are practical manuals for managers and policy makers. A new orthodoxy is in the making, an orthodoxy in which it becomes taken for granted that "knowledge"is the only source of value, that work is contingent and delocalizable, that globalization is an inexorable and inevitable process and that, by implication, resistance is futile and any assertion of the physical claims of the human body in the here-and-now is hopelessly old-fashioned. The implications of this emerging "common sense" are immense. Capable of shaping issues as diverse as taxation, employment legislation, levels of welfare spending, privacy rights, and environmental policy, these notions serve to legitimize a new political agenda and set the scene for a new phase of capital accumulation.

The task I have set myself in this essay is to re-embody cyberspace: to try to make visible the material components of this virtual world. In this, I find myself rather oddly positioned. Having been arguing for over two decades for greater importance to be given in economic and social analysis to white-collar employment, and to the ways in which information and communications technologies have facilitated its relocation, it seems perverse, to say the least, to respond to this sudden new interest in the subject by saying, in effect, "Well, hang on a minute. Are things really changing all that much? How 'dematerialized' are most developed economies? To what extent is service employment really expanding? What contribution does 'knowledge' make to economic growth? And how global are most economies anyway?"

In addressing such questions a delicate path has to be picked. On the one hand, it is necessary to subject the claims of the proponents of the "new economics" to some empirical tests. Before throwing out the bath water, in other words, it is wise to check it for babies. On the other hand, it is necessary to avoid the opposite danger of assuming that nothing has changed: that because something cannot be measured accurately with existing instruments it does not exist at all. I cannot claim to have walked this path to its conclusion. However, I hope to have flagged some of the more important land mines to be avoided along the way. If I have not found solutions, I hope I have at least identified some problems.[2]

At the risk of appearing pretentious, it does seem necessary to set the problem in its epistemological context. The current hegemonic position of postmodernism in most university departments (with the partial exception of the "hard" sciences) has created a number of obstacles to addressing such questions.[3]

First, and most obviously, postmodernism throws into question the very scientific project itself. Even to admit to trying to discover the "truth" about what is happening is to run the risk of being accused of vulgar positivism. If one accepts that all facts are contingent and socially constructed there is no rational basis for even selecting the data with which to test an argument, let alone for claiming any special validity for one's own discoveries. This is not the place for a detailed discussion of how—or indeed whether—it is possible for a scholar to find a third route, which avoids both the hard rocks of crude positivism and the swampy morass of relativism to which such an approach inevitably leads.[4]

Second, by insisting that all science is socially constructed, postmodernism makes it very difficult to produce a stable concept of the body—the flesh-and-blood body that gets on with the business of circulating its blood, digesting, perspiring, shedding old cells, lactating, producing semen, menstruating, and myriad other functions (including, no doubt, many that a positivist might describe as "yet to be discovered") regardless of what its inhabitant is thinking. The problem is urgent: how to resolve the crude dualism that is set up when "the biological" is counterposed to "the social" (or "nature" to "culture," "body" to "mind," "manual work" to "mental work," "the material" to the "ideological," that which is studied to the scientist, and so on). But postmodernism has yet to produce a definitive resolution to this difficulty. Baudrillard's solution is to regard the human body itself as just another culturally constructed simulacrum.[5] An alternative model, proposed by Donna Haraway, is to acknowledge the ways in which science and technology have penetrated the natural by proposing that the body cannot be viewed independently from its cultural surroundings but has, in effect, become a cyborg.[6] In both of these approaches the body is reduced to a cultural construct, which has the effect of rendering its materiality difficult to grasp and analyze. This is relevant in this context because without a concept of the body as something distinct and separate from capital (or any other abstraction) any theorizing about the weightless economy will be circular: one is, in effect, trying to see the place of labor in the capital accumulation process having already written out the possibility of being able to define (and measure) that labor.

The postmodernist approach has also led to a third problem, which is pertinent in this context: the conception of "culture" as series of discourses, endlessly renegotiated and reproduced by all those who participate in them. This, combined with the focus on semiotic analysis to analyze these discourses, makes invisible the fact that cultural products such as books, films, "science," or advertisements—and the "ideas" they contain (at least to the extent that these are a conscious result of mental effort) are also the products of human intellectual and physical labor. Without some means of modeling, and measuring, this labor (whether waged or not), it is extremely difficult to make analytical sense of the "weightless economy."

Having outlined some of the difficulties, let us go on to examine the main tenets of the "weightless economy" school. Three quite distinct themes emerge in this literature: dematerialization; the "productivity paradox," and globalization. Although these are capable of being separated from one another conceptually, they tend in practice to be discussed together.

One of the leading proponents of the dematerialization thesis is Danny Quah, a Harvard-trained econometrician who is a professor at the London School of Economics.[7] His central argument is that the economy is becoming increasingly dematerialized with intangible services increasingly replacing physical goods as the main sources of value. He distinguishes two aspects of dematerialization that he regards as having macroeconomic importance: "The first is simply increased weightlessness deriving from the growth of services—as opposed to, say, manufacturing in particular, or industry in general. The second is dematerialization deriving from the increased importance of IT."[8]

Let us look first at the growth in services. It has been an article of faith in most of the literature, at least since Daniel Bell first coined the term "postindustrial society" in the early 1970s, that a major, if not *the* major trend of the twentieth century has been the rise of services at the expense of agriculture and manufacturing.[9] The most usual measure of this rise is service employment, and it is readily illustrated by graphs (usually derived from census data) showing employment in services soaring heavenward as the century progresses, while employment in agriculture and manufacturing falls dramatically. Before going on to a more detailed discussion of service employment, it is worth noting several difficulties with this representation.

First, the standard industrial classification system, which is used as a basis for assigning workers to sectors, fails to take account of the major changes in the division of labor that accompany technological change and the restructuring of economic activity, both in terms of ownership and of organization. Thus, for instance, the "decline" of agricultural employment, which is visible in terms of the numbers of people actually working on the land, can only be demonstrated by leaving the mechanization of farming and the commodification of food production out of the picture. If you were to include, for example, all the people employed in making tractors, fertilizers, and pesticides, and all the people engaged in packing and preparing food, and those involved in its distribution to supermarkets as part of the agricultural workforce, the graph would slope much less steeply. Similarly, the decline in manufacturing employment is usually demonstrated within a particular national context, or that of a group of nations (for instance the OECD nations, the countries covered by NAFTA, or the EU). This fails to take account of the manufacturing employment that has simply been relocated to another part of the globe (although it may still be carried out by the same companies, based in the same countries and retaining their service employment there). Finally, the growth in service employment over the course of the century can only be demonstrated convincingly by leaving out domestic servants, whose numbers have declined steadily as employment in other forms of service work has risen.[10] In Great Britain, for instance, domestic service accounted for 40 percent of all female employment in 1901, but had fallen to 5.2 percent by 1971.[11]

These qualifications aside, there are deeper difficulties involved. Any analysis that uses as its raw material aggregated data on "service activities," whether these are derived from employment statistics, output data, or other sources, is in effect collapsing together several quite different types of economic activity, involving contrasting and contradictory tendencies. While it may be possible to make a case that dematerialization is taking place in some of these, it is my contention that in others precisely the opposite tendency is occurring, and that in the long run this tendency of commodification, or the transformation of services into material products, is the dominant one in capitalism.

The aggregated category "services," which Quah and others use as the basis for their calculations, can be broken down into three distinct types of activity. The first of these consists essentially of a socialization of the kinds of work that are also carried out unpaid in the home or neighborhood. This work includes health care, child care, social work, cleaning, catering, and a range of personal services like hairdressing. It also includes what one might call "public housekeeping," such as the provision of leisure services, street cleaning, refuse collection, or park keeping. Even "live" entertainment— and the sex industry—can plausibly be included in this category. (Under the standard industrial classification scheme, or SIC, it is mostly classified under "hotels, catering, retail and wholesale distribution," "miscellaneous services" or in the public sector, although it is not coterminous with these categories.)

Whether or not outputs from these activities or employment in these sectors are visible in the economic statistics varies and depends on a number of factors including demographic structure, the degree of political commitment to providing public services, cultural variations, the extent of female participation in the workforce, and what Gøsta Esping-Andersen has described as "de-commodification," defined as "the degree to which individuals or families can uphold a socially acceptable standard of living independently of market participation."[12] These activities become visible in the public accounts when they are first socialized and enter the money economy: when, for instance, it becomes possible to attend a public concert instead of singing around the piano at home, to take an ailing baby to a clinic, or to get one's legs waxed at a beauty salon. Conversely, they revert to invisibility if they are not available in the market. If, for instance, a political decision were made to abandon the state provision of school meals, employment of school meals staff would decline, but this would not necessarily mean that the labor of preparing such meals had disappeared; it would in all likelihood simply have reentered the sphere of unpaid domestic work.

I have argued elsewhere (see Chapter 5) that it is not simply the boundary between paid and unpaid labor that is permeable and shifting; this kind of "service" activity is also in an active process of commodification.[13] The general tendency is for new technologies to be used, not to dematerialize these activities but to materialize them (albeit in some cases with more and more "knowledge" embedded in the new commodities). Thus we have a historical progression from washing clothes in the home as an activity either carried out unpaid or by the labor of paid domestic servants, via the provision of public laundries (staffed by "service" workers) back into the home where it is now once again generally carried out as unpaid work but using an ever-burgeoning variety of new commodities such as washing machines, detergents, tumble dryers, fabric conditioners, and steam irons. These undeniably material goods are made in factories and transported physically from these factories by various means to a growing proportion of homes throughout the world. The need to purchase these goods serves as one of the many ties pulling the "underdeveloped" portions of that world ever more tightly into the cash nexus.

Washing, of course, is not the only activity that has been commodified in this way. One could point with equal justification to the processed food industry or the drugs industry as examples of commodified domestic labor. A random perusal of the advertisements in the room as I write this article throws up "lunch-box-sized individual fruit-flavored portions of fromage frais" (packaged in foil tubes!), "panty-liners with flexible wings," "under-eye moisturizer," and a "universal remote control." Not only can all of these commodities be traced readily back to their origins in unsocialized activity, but it would also be fair to say that none of them, with the possible exception of the moisturizer, would have been conceivable a generation ago. The ability of capitalism to generate new commodities can seem almost magical, as though they are being conjured out of the air in a perfect reversal of the "dematerialization" hypothesis. We must remind ourselves, however, that their raw materials come from the earth and that the only magic involved is human inventiveness and labor.

A few statistics on the consumption of these raw materials underline the point: in the United Kingdom, iron consumption has increased twenty-fold since 1900; the global production of aluminium has risen from 1.5 million tons in 1950 to 20 million tons today.[14] In the decade 1984–1995 (during a period in which we should have seen the "weightless" effect becoming visible, if the theorists are to be believed) aluminum consumption in the U.K. rose from 497,000 tons to 636,000; steel consumption increased from 14,330,000 to 15,090,000 tons; and wood and paper consumption more than doubled, from 41 million to 93 million tons.[15]

This inexorable drive toward the creation of new commodities is perhaps the central drive in the history of capitalism; the physical production of material goods being the simplest way of deriving value from living labor. It is not, of course, the only way. There are profits to be made, for instance, from running private nursing homes, or contract cleaning agencies, from servicing computers, arranging conferences, or organizing rock concerts. However, partly because of the limitations on the extent to which human productivity in these areas can be enhanced by automation and the consequent dependence on a geographically fixed and skill-specific workforce, it is easier and in the long run more profitable to be in the business of manufacturing and/or distributing endlessly reproducible material commodities. Thus while most of the major opera houses in the world require a public subsidy to stay open, selling *Pavarotti's Greatest Hits* on CD is hugely lucrative. Similarly, commodified medicine, in the form of mass sales of patented drugs, seems likely to remain much more profitable than employing doctors and nurses. These products do "contain" knowledge (in the first case in the form of the composer's score, the performance of the conductor, orchestra, and singer, the skills of the producer and studio engineers, the intellectual labor of the scientists and technicians who developed recording technology in general and CD technology in particular, and so on; in the second case *inter alia* in the form of inputs from doctors, scientific researchers, and laboratory technicians). Except where this knowledge is paid for on a royalty basis, this can be regarded as "dead" labor, whose cost is amortized in the early stages of production, producing a steadily increasing profit margin that grows with the size of the production run.

We can see, therefore, that in at least some parts of the service sector, the trend is one of materialization, rather than dematerialization. What of the others?

A second category of service activity could be classified as the development of human capital—the reproduction of the knowledge workforce itself. Into this category come education and training and some kinds of research and development. This sector is not immune from commodification—witness the standardization of courses and the development of products such as interactive CD-ROMs to deliver instruction. David Noble has argued that the introduction of intranets (a series of computers linked together on an internal telecommunications network) into universities is ushering in a new era of commodification in higher education. Noble argues that both the research and the teaching functions of the universities are being commodified; witness the transformation of scientific knowledge into marketable products and the proliferation of Web-based courses and educational software.[16]

The content of these new commodities is abstract, in the sense that it has been abstracted from the lecturers, researchers, and graduate students employed in this sector. Unlike past forms of commodified scholarship, such as textbooks, these newer means of abstraction rarely acknowledge the authors' ownership by means of royalties. Nevertheless, they do not differ fundamentally from the process whereby the design of a carpet is abstracted from a skilled weaver and embedded in the programming instructions for an automated loom. What it is important to keep sight of here is that the workforce has not disappeared. Even if the more original and creative (and perhaps hence the most troublesome) workers could somehow be emptied of all the knowledge that their employers find useful and got rid of, a workforce—including original and creative people—would still be required, however deskilled and intensified the rest of the work process had become, to replenish the stock of intellectual capital, produce new educational commodities, and administer the new standardized courses, in standardized doses, to the next generation of students.

The systematization of education that has taken place in recent years bears a close resemblance to the systematization of other forms of non-manual work. For instance, the way in which the assessment of students' work may be transformed from a mystified and subjective process of exercising individual professional judgment to the ticking of boxes on a standard marking scheme is not unlike the way a bank manager's assessment of a client's eligibility for a loan or mortgage increasingly turns on the administration of a standard questionnaire, with standard built-in criteria, in which the decision is effectively made by the software program.

This sector, then, is one where enormous changes are taking place in the labor process (and, with it, the capital accumulation process) in association with the introduction of the new information technologies. It does not, however, appear to raise any new problems that are not soluble within the framework of the "old" economics.

The third category of service activity is the one that most concerns Quah and the other economists of the "weightless" school. This is the "knowledge work" that is either directly involved in the production of physical commodities or involved in the production of new commodities that are entirely weightless. In the former category, an oft-cited example is that of the fashion shoe, only a fraction of the price of which is attributable to the raw materials and the cost of physical manufacture and transport. The main value, it is argued, comes from the "weightless" attributes of the shoe, derived from its design, its brand image, the way in which it is marketed and so on. As Diane Coyle puts it, the "buyer is paying for what they do for her image rather than something to protect her feet."[17] Notwithstanding the extra money a purchaser is prepared to pay for a high status product, it is still, at the end of a day, a material object being purchased, from which the manufacturers derive their profit. The snob value of a Nike running shoe in the 1990s is not different *in kind* from that of a sought-after Paris bonnet in the nineteenth century; the main difference lies in the fact that the former is mass-produced while the latter was individually made.[18] In the former case, the "knowledge" has been abstracted from a specialist knowledge worker in a reproducible form; in the second it lay embedded in the skill of the milliner whose bodily presence was thus required to produce each new bonnet.

The emergence of the specialist knowledge worker is thus a product of the increasingly specialized division of labor in manufacturing.[19] In this process, as the physical business of production becomes more and more capital intensive, through automation, the manual processes of assembly become progressively deskilled, enabling the work to be done ever more cheaply. In the case of sports shoes, this is often by the use of extremely low-paid labor in developing countries. In 1995, for instance, it was reported that 12,000 women were employed in Indonesia making Nike shoes, working sixty hours a week and many earning less than the government's minimum wage of $1.80 a day. It was estimated that raising their wages to $3.50 per day would still bring the labor cost component of a pair of shoes to less than $1 a pair. In 1993, by contrast, Michael Jordan alone received over $20 million from Nike for allowing his name and image (and by implication his sporting achievements) to be associated with their product—equivalent to more than the total labor cost for all the 19 million pairs of Nike shoes made in Indonesia.[20] Traditional economics allows us to understand the very small proportion of the cost of the final shoe attributable to the labor involved in its manufacture as the super-exploitation of a vulnerable group of workers; the "new" economics simply renders them invisible. Yet it is difficult to see the division of labor in the production process as anything intrinsically new; rather it can be seen as the continuation of a process that has been evolving for at least the past century and a half.[21] Michael Jordan may be earning considerably more, but his contribution to the value of the final product is not different *in kind* from that of the little girls who posed for the Pears Soap advertisements at the turn of the century or the members of the royal family who give their official blessing and the use of their coats of arms to pots of marmalade.[22]

What is perhaps new is the large-scale introduction of new technologies not just into the process of *production* of commodities but also into their *distribution*. The creation of global markets for mass-produced commodities has generated imperatives to increase the efficiency of this distribution workforce and, indeed, to introduce entirely new ways of reaching potential customers and persuade them to buy. In some cases this has produced the rather paradoxical effect of re-creating the illusion of a return to the customization of products associated with the era before mass production. Thus, for instance, there are now websites into which you can input your measurements to enable you to order a pair of jeans tailored to your own precise individual dimensions (provided, of course, you are prepared to select from a menu of standard styles from a single manufacturer). The computerization of parts of the production process has been combined with the use of the new communications technologies to create a direct interactive link between customer and producer. This also has the effect of cutting out various intermediaries (such as the wholesaler and the retailer) and of reducing the manufacturer's risk of overproducing, or producing the wrong product, almost to zero: only that which has already been ordered by the customer need ever be produced. In this case, however, there is still a material commodity that has to be manufactured, packed, and delivered over real physical distances to its customer.

In other cases, the commodity being distributed is less easy to pin down in its material form. An example of this might be the use of a call center for activities like selling airline tickets, providing directory inquiry information, arranging financial transactions, providing assistance on software problems, or dealing with insurance claims. Again, the sophisticated use of new technology makes it possible to personalize these services, however remote the site from which they are delivered. Software can, for instance, be programmed to use the area code from which a call is originated to direct the caller to an operator who will reply in the right language or even the appropriate regional accent, thus creating an illusion of local response whatever the actual location or time zone. The same digital trigger (the caller's telephone number) can also be used to ensure that the caller's personal file is visible on the screen to the operator before the first "hello" has even been uttered, making it possible to generate a highly personalized response and, indeed, an illusion of intimacy, as well as maximizing the operator's productivity by avoiding any waste of time in taking down unnecessary details.

The use of computer-generated scripts that pop up on the screen to be read verbatim by the operator can reduce the skill requirements to a minimum. This sort of work is also amenable to a high degree of remote monitoring and control. Studies of call center workers in the United Kingdom—already an estimated 1.1 percent of the workforce in a market estimated to be growing at the rate of 32 percent per annum across Europe—have found that the work is highly controlled, relatively low-paid, frequently involves round-the-clock shift working and produces a rapid rate of staff turnover, with "burn-out" typically occurring after twelve to twenty months on the job.[23] The evidence suggests that, far from constituting some

new kind of knowledge worker, formerly unknown to economics, these are
the Taylorized, deskilled descendants of earlier forms of office worker (such
as bank tellers, insurance salespeople, booking clerks, and telephone operators) even though the work may be taking place at different locations and
under different conditions of employment. There seems to be no good
reason why the value they add to the products or services being delivered
(which may or may not be of a tangible nature) cannot also be measured by
the traditional means.

This brings us to the other kind of knowledge work in this category
discussed in the "weightless economy" literature—the kind that produces
no material end-product whatsoever. This may take the form of algorithms
(such as a software program), intangible financial products (such as a life
insurance policy), creative works (such as a film script), or speculations (such
as an investment in futures). Again, none of these is new in itself: a musical
score, the perforated roll of paper that contains the "instructions" for a
pianola, a chemical formula, the blueprint for a machine, or indeed a recipe
book represent essentially the same kind of algorithm as a computer
program. And various forms of gambling, usury, and insurance seem to have
been around for as long as money. In the seventeenth century, one of the
earliest uses of official statistics (in this case the *London Bills of Mortality*,
from which the merchant John Graunt constructed life expectancy tables)
was for the calculation of annuities.[24] And writers, poets, dramatists, visual
artists, scientists, inventors, and musicians have been producing "intangible
products" for centuries. When we read of rock musicians borrowing money
on the world's stock markets against their future royalty earnings, this may
seem like some new semi-magical way of generating income out of thin air,
but is it really very different from the way in which impecunious young
aristocrats in the eighteenth century settled their gambling debts by the use
of IOUs drawn against their future inheritance? Danny Quah argues that
weightless products defy the traditional laws of economics because they are
simultaneously infinitely expandable, indivisible, and inappropriable. In
other words, a new idea can only be discovered once; once discovered it can
be used over and over again without being "used up." And even if there are
formal restrictions, in the form of patents or copyright, on doing this, it can
in practice be freely reproduced.[25] While it is certainly true that the new

communications and reproductive technologies have made the rapid dissemination of ideas easier than ever before, this again does not appear to be a new phenomenon. Surely these features have always been present when new discoveries have been made (such as the use of penicillin to heal infection, or the theory of gravity, or the discovery of electricity). And the copying of ideas is as old as the history of fashion.

It is possible to argue about the exact relationship of these abstract products to material reality. In some cases they may act as proxies for material goods (as in the case of a mortgage, which can be exchanged for a house, or an insurance policy that can be exchanged for a new car, or indeed a credit card transaction that can be exchanged for goods or cash). In other cases (for instance, in the case of a piece of music or a poem), it is more useful to envisage these products in relation to the human desires they satisfy.

If we are to avoid constructing a purely abstract universe, constituted entirely of "knowledge" (in which disembodied entities inhabit a virtual space, are sustained by virtual inputs, and produce virtual outputs—a universe without birth or death, a universe where infinite consumption is possible without the generation of waste), it is useful to retain an awareness of this underlying materiality. From an economic perspective, I would argue, it is important to retain a more specific awareness of the materiality of the worker and his or her labor process. It is only by examining this process in some detail that it becomes possible to tease out the specific contributions made at each stage to the "value" of the final commodity. Such an analysis can also illuminate the process that Marx identified whereby labor is progressively abstracted and incorporated into capital in its specific relation to "knowledge" work in an economy increasingly dependent on the use of information and communications technologies.

In brief, we could say that in the 1990s the division of labor evolved to a point where a substantial part of the labor force is engaged in "non-manual" work—in the generation or processing of "information" (even though this work nevertheless involves the body in a series of physical activities, such as pounding a keyboard, that have implications for its physiological well-being). The development of computing technology has made it possible for this information to be digitized and for some aspects of its processing to be automated, and the development of telecommunications technology has enabled this digital information to be transmitted from one place to another with great rapidity and at very low cost. These technologies in combination have made it possible for many of these processes to be standardized, as a result of which it has become possible for the workers to be monitored by results, and for the task to be relocated to any point on the globe where the right infrastructure is available together with a workforce with the appropriate skills.

We must now ask ourselves what, precisely, is the relationship of this workforce to capital? How is the value of the final commodity constituted? In relation to its material content, Marx has already given us the answer: there is the dead labor of past workers embodied in the machinery used to make it, and in the extraction of the raw materials and the capital used to set the enterprise up, and the appropriated living labor of the workers who process it. In relation to the intangible content, there is also the dead labor of the people whose past work made the idea possible, but there is also living labor in two quite distinct forms.[26] The first of these is the routine labor of deskilled workers who are essentially following instructions. We might call these "process" knowledge workers. These may be involved either in the production process (for instance, coders working on the development of software, graphic designers laying out Web pages, copy typists inputting data, managers supervising the purchasing of raw materials or the organization of the production process, quality controllers checking the final output) or in the distribution process (such as call center staff or invoice clerks). Although when it is casualized some form of payment by results (or piece rate) may be applied, it is normally paid by time, as is the case with manual work. Even if the activity is outsourced, the wage or salary bill is verifiable and it is thus a relatively straightforward task to relate these labor costs to the output in order to calculate the value added.

Then there is also another kind of knowledge work, which we might call "creative" or "originating" labor (some of which may be contributed, with or without acknowledgment, by the "process" workers), that generates new intellectual capital, in the form of ideas, designs, programs, or more definable (if not tangible) intellectual products such as words, music, or images. The contribution made by this work is harder to calculate. The ideas may be appropriated from a waged workforce (in most countries, ownership of intellectual property produced by employees is automatically assigned to the employer). However, they may be produced by freelancers or other independent individuals or organizations under agreements that assign all or part of the ownership of rights to the creator. In such cases, the right to use the intellectual product may involve the payment of fees or royalties or the negotiation of complex licensing agreements. Alternatively, the ideas may simply be stolen. Intellectual property rights can be legally asserted not just in the outputs of workers who are conscious of their role as generators of valuable ideas—for instance, as writers, artists, or inventors—but they also apply to the tacit knowledge of people who have no awareness of the alienable nature of what they own. The music of tribal peoples, for example, may be appropriated to be used on CDs or film soundtracks; their visual art may be photographed and printed on T-shirts or wrapping paper, or scanned in to give an "ethnic" feel to the design of a Web page; their sacred artifacts may be used as "inspiration" for a new range of designer clothes or jewelry. It does not stop there: supermarkets developing "ethnic" convenience foods will generally insist that the subcontractors who prepare the food for them give them an exclusive right to use the recipe; the handed-down knowledge of the family or community thus becomes appropriated as privately owned intellectual capital.[27] Even more extreme is the patenting of human genetic codes for research purposes, a development of the practice of patenting the DNA of various plants and animals (with a slight tweak to ensure its uniqueness) for use in new drugs and genetic engineering products.[28]

It is no accident that the ownership of intellectual property is currently one of the most hotly contended issues both at the level of international trade agreements and the level of workplace negotiation. In the United Kingdom, for instance, the National Union of Journalists has found itself in recent years in a series of disputes with large employers over the right of freelance journalists and photographers to retain ownership of copyright for their own work. Many employers, including the supposedly left-of-center *Guardian* newspaper, now make it a condition of employment that all rights, electronic or otherwise, become the property of the newspaper.[29] On one level, this can be regarded as a simple dispute between labor and capital, with workers fighting for a larger share of the products of their labor.

However, the concept of ownership is rather different from that which pertains in a typical factory. It is now over two centuries since workers effectively gave up their right to a share in the ownership of the product of their labor in return for a wage. The knowledge workers who insist on a royalty, or on the right to reuse what they have produced, are not behaving like members of the proletariat; they are refusing alienation.

Nevertheless, the worker's right to ownership of the "idea" (as opposed to the right to be paid for the time put in on the processing of that idea) is profoundly ambiguous. The knowledge worker usually occupies an intermediate position in what might be seen as the knowledge food chain. Ideas do not come from nowhere: they may be copied, consciously or unconsciously, from others; they may draw on what has been learned from teachers, or from books, or from observations of people who do not regard themselves as creative; or ideas may arise from the interactions of a group of people working together as a team. A journalist or television researcher generally obtains inputs from interviews with "experts" (who may or may not be salaried academics or writers with an interest in plugging their books); there is no rational basis for deciding whether the end result should "belong" to the journalist's employer, the journalist, the "expert," or someone further down the chain; for example, the "expert's" research assistant, or a person interviewed by the research assistant in the course of carrying out the research, or indeed the parents of the person interviewed by the research assistant who inculcated the views expressed in the interview. An analogous intermediary position could be said to be occupied by the scientist doing research on disease resistance in rice who obtains information from Southeast Asian peasants as part of the process that eventually leads to his or her employer registering a claim to ownership of the new strain that is developed; or by Paul Simon incorporating tribal music into "his" work; or by the photographer who records the face of an elderly Jamaican fisherman to use to advertise a canned drink.

In the final analysis it is market strength that determines who can claim what share of the cake, but the analysis of how the "value" is formed is complicated by these considerations. The fact that it is complicated to model does not render the task impossible. In order to do so, it is necessary to take account of the fact that real people with real bodies have contributed real time to the development of these "weightless" commodities.

This brings me to the second issue that occupies such a large place in the weightless economy literature: the so-called productivity paradox. The starting point for this discussion is the belief that growth rates, measured in gross domestic product (GDP) and total factor productivity (TFP) have in most developed countries remained obstinately low since 1973— well below their postwar levels to that date. This year is chosen as the watershed partly because it was in 1973 that the oil crisis generated a number of dramatic hiccups in the economic statistics, and partly because it more or less coincided with the beginnings of what has been various described as the "knowledge economy," the "information economy," the "second industrial revolution," or the "computer revolution." If, as is widely argued on both the Left and the Right of the political spectrum, the introduction of these new technologies can unleash human potential, making workers more productive and creating a host of new products and services, then this ought to have led to a surge in economic growth. The apparent evidence that it has not is one of the main factors leading to the belief that a new economics is required. However, the paradox may not be as surprising as it first appears.

First, the evidence itself: productivity is normally measured by the relationship between the value of outputs and that of the inputs of labor and capital. As Danny Quah has pointed out, if we are to judge by the statistics alone, the most productive group of workers in the world are French farmers.[30] The implication is that apparently high productivity can simply be an effect of artificially high prices of final outputs. This suggests that part of the explanation for the "productivity paradox" may lie in the very sharp reduction in prices that has accompanied the process of computerization.

But do the empirical data support this definition of the problem? In this connection, Neuburger has convincingly shown that although there was a sharp drop in *output*, labor productivity did not exhibit a correspondingly sharp fall, and in some OECD countries did not fall significantly at all.[31] Moreover, for the United Kingdom he has also shown that the present system of public accounts would only reveal the kind of productivity gains delivered by information technology in about 10 percent of the sectors comprising the total economy.[32] Nonetheless, a paradox does seem to exist, even if not in nearly as extreme a form as generally supposed. So what might be the explanation for it? Is political economy really incapable of providing one? Here I can only indicate some of the main possible solutions to the puzzle out of the many that have been proposed. One has to do with the effects of globalization. It is difficult for nationally based systems of accounting to deal accurately with the transactions taking place in a globalized economy. Where high levels of output are recorded in one country, but some of the inputs may have been in the form of very cheap labor in another, and complex adjustments have to be made to allow for such factors as fluctuating exchange rates and transfer pricing practices within large transnational companies, then some slippage may take place that affects the GDP figures positively or negatively.

There are also many ways in which the extra productivity produced by information technology may not reveal itself in output figures. It may increase the efficiency of *unpaid* rather than paid labor; for example, by making it much quicker and easier for a library user to identify a book or a customer to withdraw cash from a bank. To the extent that information technology encourages the development of self-service this will not be reflected in the figures. It could be argued that a firm that improves its service to customers will thereby gain market share and this will ultimately feed through into increased output figures, but this does not take account of the generalized effect that takes place when the whole sector has adopted this new technology; customer expectations will have risen but no single firm has a competitive advantage. In addition, Jeff Madrick has raised a number of other technical issues, including a possible oversupply of services, that may have affected the statistics in the United States.[33]

There are also specific problems associated with the public sector: improvements in efficiency and quality of service resulting from the introduction of new technologies into public administration or the delivery of public services may well lead to a better quality of life, but this will not be reflected in the output figures, since national accounts do not at present capture in any direct way things like cleaner air, healthier children, happier cyclists, or less confused form fillers. It is sometimes argued that the nature of Britain's publicly funded National Health Service creates a consistent bias in the national accounts leading to an underestimation of GDP.

A study of the public sector also raises some more fundamental questions relating to the socialization of domestic labor (discussed above in the context of service employment). Part of the apparent fall in productivity from the 1970s onward might be a direct effect of the greater labor force participation of women during that period, and hence an increase in the need for a market supply of child care and other services previously provided in the home.[34] A group of Norwegian researchers used a social accounting framework to decompose GDP growth into productivity gains and "reallocation" gains resulting from the transition from unpaid household production to the labor market. They concluded that "about one-fourth of the growth in GDP in Norway over the period 1971–1990 can be attributed to the transition of household services from unpaid to paid work."[35]

Neuburger"s own explanation for the "productivity paradox," insofar as it exists, is an interesting one. He hypothesizes that during the 1970s there was a qualitative improvement in working conditions across most of the OECD countries and that the increased cost of inputs (reflected in lower productivity growth figures) represented a real gain for labor, in the form of improved health and safety at work, a better working environment, longer holidays, and other achievements. In most developed countries, 1970–1976 was, after all, as well as being a time of considerable trade union militancy, the period in which equal pay, protection against discrimination, maternity rights, protection against unfair dismissal, the right to a safe working environment, and a number of other rights were, at least formally, enshrined in employment protection or anti-discrimination legislation. Although much of the legislation was difficult to implement and many workers fell through the net it did, according to Neuburger, lead to some measurable redistribution from capital to labor, and the productivity figures provide the evidence for it.

These issues of productivity and growth are, then, evidently complex. However, we can at least conclude that they cannot be understood in relation to technology alone but must be analyzed in their full social and historical context.

A third strand in the discussions about the weightless economy concerns globalization. Perhaps one of the most dangerous illusions fostered here is the notion that the new information technologies mean that anything can now be done by anyone, anywhere, that the entire population of the globe has become a potential virtual workforce. The issue of globalization is crucial because it raises directly the question of how the virtual economy, insofar as it exists, maps on to the physical surface of the globe we inhabit.

Although it is full of euphemistic descriptions of the "death of distance" or the "end of geography," the literature on the subject is surprisingly short on empirical evidence.[36] At one extreme, skeptics such as Paul Hirst and Grahame Thompson go so far as to assert that a global economy cannot be said to exist in any meaningful sense, and even maintain that the world economy is somewhat *less* global now than it was before the First World War.[37] At the other extreme is a large literature, much of it by postmodernist geographers, which takes the presumption that globalization is taking place as its starting point and is concerned with developing an understanding of the social, cultural, and economic implications of this. The empirical evidence on which it draws is, however, slight, rarely going beyond the anecdote or case-study writ large.[38] Few systematic attempts have been made to establish the scale of relocation of information-processing work across national boundaries.

It is extraordinarily difficult to obtain a statistical picture of the changing international division of labor. Apart from the difficulty of distinguishing between final outputs and intermediate ones, the traffic in jobs will not necessarily even appear in an easily identifiable form in the trade statistics, because of the range of different contractual arrangements that might apply, each of which is visible in a different way in the national accounts. Material goods must be transported in a physical form across national boundaries and are therefore generally recorded in import and export statistics; but information sent over the Internet leaves no such trace and there is no easy way to assess the value of such traffic. It is, of course, possible to measure its *volume* but, despite the arguments of Luc Soete and others who propose a "bit tax," this is not a good indicator of value: a computer program that has taken thousands of skilled person-hours to write will typically be much smaller in volume (measured in bits) than a video clip or scanned-in photograph in whose generation only a few moments of unpaid time have been invested.[39]

The fact that something is difficult to measure does not mean that it does not exist, and it is clear that the widespread use of computers for processing information, and of telecommunications for transmitting it, *has* introduced an enormous new range of choices in the location of information-processing work.

However, it would not be correct to infer from this that these choices are entirely untethered from the material. First, and most obviously, they depend on a physical infrastructure. The process that was formalized in the liberalization of the telecommunications market following the ratification of the World Trade Organization pact of February 15, 1997, by sixty-eight countries has opened up most of the world as a market for the major telecommunications multinationals and involves a rapid spread of infrastructure and a sharp fall in telecommunications costs. But this process has been highly selective; it certainly cannot be said to have given all the world's population access to the "information society." In many developing countries whole communities are effectively without telephone access, and even those lines that exist are of poor quality. The fiber optical cable required to transmit high volumes of information quickly, and which provides a vital underpinning for many "weightless" activities, is so far only available in selected parts of the globe, mainly in large cities, such as Singapore, where high usage, and hence profitability, is anticipated.

Even "wireless" communications are dependent on material goods, like satellites, to continue functioning. On May 20, 1998, Americans were reminded sharply of this when there was a malfunction in the onboard control system and a backup switch of the Galaxy IV satellite, owned by PanAmSat. The satellite reportedly provided pager service to more than 80 percent of U.S. pager users and also carried National Public Radio, several television networks, and Reuters news feeds. While CBS services were quickly switched to Galaxy 7, pager users, including many hospitals, were left without any service.[40]

Telecommunications infrastructure is not the only material prerequisite for participation in the global weightless economy. There is also a need, continuously renewed because of its rapid obsolescence, for hardware: personal computers, mobile telephones, modems, scanners, printers, switches, and the many components and accessories involved in their manufacture and use. Not only do the costs of these differ in absolute terms from country to country, but so does their cost relative to basic income and subsistence. Mike Holderness has pointed out that "a reasonable computer costs about one year's unemployment benefit in the United Kingdom or about the annual income of three schoolteachers in Calcutta" and that the annual subscription to Ghana's only Internet host is about the same as the entire annual income of a Ghanaian journalist.[41]

The notion that anyone can do anything anywhere is therefore in practice constrained by a number of spatial factors. It is also, of course, constrained by the fact that not all human activities are delocalizable in this way. The majority of jobs are, and seem likely to remain, firmly anchored to a given spot, or series of spots, on the world's surface because they involve the extraction of the earth's raw materials, their processing, the manufacture of material commodities (which is delocalizable, but within limits), transport, construction, or the delivery of physical services (ranging from health care to garbage collection).

That said, it is undeniably the case that more and more work *is* delocalizable. The reasons for this are many. First, there are the changes in the division of labor that have increased the proportion of jobs that simply involve processing information. Second, the digitization of that information has vastly increased the extent to which it can be accessed remotely, removing the need for physical proximity to sources and eliminating transport costs. Third, the standardization of tasks associated with computerization has enabled a growing proportion of activities to be monitored remotely (replacing management of the work process with management by results), which in turn allows them to be outsourced or located at a distance from the manager. Fourth—partly because of the hegemonic power of companies like IBM and Microsoft—there has been a convergence of skill requirements across occupations and industries, with a few generic skills (such as a knowledge of Microsoft Word or Excel) replacing a large number of machine-specific, firm-specific, or occupation-specific skills that have in the past both constrained the mobility of workers and created a dependence on their skills among employers, effectively anchoring them to the places where those skills were available. Fifth, as already noted, there has been both a rapid diffusion of the infrastructure and technology and a sharp fall in its cost.[42]

This should, in principle, have enabled any region in which the right combination of infrastructure and skills is present to diversify its local economy and enter the global market in information-processing work on an equal basis with any other region. By removing the strategic advantages of some regions (created by such things as economies of scale or proximity to markets), it should have leveled the playing field. It is this idea that underlies much of the optimistic rhetoric about the ability of new information and communications technologies to regenerate remote regions. However, the results of empirical research reveal that things are not so simple.

The very fact that employers now have a huge range of alternative locations to choose from appears, paradoxically, to have increased rather than decreased the degree of geographical segregation in the global division of labor. Although its specific components may have changed, comparative competitive advantage is more rather than less important, with each location having to compete separately for each type of activity. No longer constrained to have most of their information-processing activities on one site, corporations are now free to seek out the best location on an activity-by-activity basis, with the whole world to choose from. Thus a company might decide to get its manufacturing done in Mexico, its research and development in California, its data entry in the Philippines, its software development in India, and establish two call centers, one in New Brunswick, Canada, and one in the Netherlands. In each case, the site would be selected on the basis of the availability of skills and the advantageousness of other local labor market conditions, tax regime, etc. If the market becomes more competitive, or local workers start demanding higher wages or better conditions, or the local tax regime changes, it might switch: it might, for instance, go to Indonesia for manufacturing, to the Dominican Republic for data entry, to Russia for programming, or start using homeworkers for some of the more routine call center functions. Even within countries, this increasing geographical specialization (generally accompanied by polarization in incomes and standards of living) can be observed. Some recent research I carried out in the United Kingdom revealed a steadily growing gap between those regions that were successful in attracting high-skilled "creative" knowledge work (mostly concentrated in an affluent "green" corridor to the west of London) and those that had succeeded only in attracting routine back-office functions and call centers (almost exclusively in declining industrial areas).[43] Remote rural areas with poor infrastructure had failed to attract either type of employment.

Such findings cast serious doubt over many of the claims made by economists of the "death of distance" school. They suggest that location has actually become *more* rather than less important. Some places seem likely to be able to build on their comparative advantages to increase the gap between themselves and the rest of the world; others seem likely to be able to find niches for themselves in the new global division of labor, by exploiting things like language skills, time zone advantages, cheap labor, specialist skills, or good infrastructure; still others will be left entirely out in the cold. The dream of a fully diversified local economy in any given area seems likely to remain unrealizable except for a few privileged pockets.

And what of the future of knowledge work? It seems likely that two existing tendencies will intensify. On the one hand, there is likely to be a continuing erosion of the traditional bureaucracy with its stable hierarchies, rigid rules, orderly—if implicitly discriminatory—promotion patterns, "jobs for life," process management, and unity of time and space, in favor of an increasingly atomized and dispersed workforce, managed by results, insecure, and expected to work from any location. If they are not actually formally self-employed, this group of workers, which will include a high proportion of the "creative" knowledge workforce, will increasingly be expected to behave as if they are. On the other hand, there is likely to be the creation of what is in effect a new white-collar proletariat engaged in the more routine "process" knowledge work, closely monitored with Taylorized work processes and stressful working conditions. Geographical segregation will make it difficult for members of the second group to progress to the first.

The geographical distribution of intellectual labor (the movement of jobs to people) is only one aspect of globalization, of course. In analyzing the forms of capital accumulation that prevail as the century draws to a close, it is also important to look at the global division of labor in terms of the physical movements of migrant workers (the movement of people to jobs) and in terms of the development of mass global markets.

In order to do so, however, it is not necessary to develop a new economics of weightlessness. On the contrary, we must reinsert human beings, in all their rounded, messy, vulnerable materiality—and the complexity of their antagonistic social relations—at the very center of our analysis.

/ 10 / THE MAKING OF A CYBERTARIAT? VIRTUAL WORK IN A REAL WORLD

IT IS POSSIBLE TO ARGUE THAT IN THE AFTERMATH OF THE 1989 collapse of the Soviet Union a single global economy is in formation. As the World Trade Organization (WTO) dismantles any remaining checks on the free movement of capital, goods and services, and intellectual property between countries, transnational corporations have an open field. With the terms of employment of a growing proportion of the world's population determined either directly or indirectly by these same corporations, the conditions would seem, at last, to have arrived to render possible the fulfilment Marx's injunction at the end of the *Communist Manifesto*: "Workers of the world unite." But are there in fact any signs that a global proletariat with a common consciousness is emerging?

This essay takes as its starting point a conception of capitalism as a dynamic force whose engine proceeds by the interrelated processes of commodification and accumulation. On the one hand, it seeks insatiably for new commodities from the production of which surplus value can be extracted, and on the other, seeks new markets to fuel its voracious expansion. New commodities arise either from the drawing into the cash economy of activities which were previously carried out by unpaid labor, for gift or exchange, or by the elaboration of existing commodities. Human activities and needs thus stand at either end of the process: production and consumption. The inevitable impetus is toward a complete industrialization of the globe, with the entire population involved on the one hand in contributing toward the production or circulation of commodities and the capital accumulation process in some capacity and on the other in an ever-greater dependence on the purchase of these commodities for their survival.

The commodification process entails continuing seismic shifts in the social division of labor. This is not the place to describe in detail how, for instance, subsistence agriculture gives way to forms of farming locked into the market by the need to acquire such things as seeds, tools, and fertilizer as well as sell its produce, or how in the process new social categories are created, such as the landless rural wage laborer or the plantation manager. Or how the resulting changes in a rural economy force peasants to send their children to the city as factory workers. Or how the automation of factories leads to a growing complexity in the division of labor that generates new groups standing between the paradigmatic proletariat and bourgeoisie: the foreman, for example, or the skilled draftsman, or the purchasing manager. Or how these groups in turn are threatened or reconstituted at the next twist of technological development. Here it is enough simply to point out that their rise, or demise, affects not only the composition of the labor force—the organization of production—but also the structure of the market—the organization of consumption—since each of these groups buys commodities as well as selling its labor.

This point becomes particularly relevant when we come to discuss the current wave of technological change—the widespread use of information and communication technologies (ICTs) —because these, unusually in the history of automation, are technologies both of production and of consumption. The possession or lack of these technologies is therefore likely to create a major new fault line running through entire populations. The "digital divide" is the currently fashionable term for this fault line.

But before examining these new demographics in detail, it is necessary to take a step back and define what it is we are talking about, by no means an easy task.

While thinking about this essay, I wrote in a newsletter:

Recent work has raised in a very acute form the problem of how to name the kinds of work that involve telematics. Even the traditional terms are unsatisfactory. "'White collar" implies a particular kind of male office worker who probably ceased being typical (if he ever was) sometime in the 1950s. "Non-manual" denies the physical reality of pounding a keyboard all day. "Office work" links it to a particular kind of location when the whole point of recent developments is that they mean such work can be done anywhere. And most of the newer terms are even worse. "Telecommuter" applies only to those people who have substituted one kind of location (the home) for another (the city center office). "Teleworker" again tends to be restricted in practice to those workers who have relocated and cannot be applied to that whole class of workers whose work is *potentially* delocalizable. Some commentators have come up with categories like "digital analyst" or "knowledge worker" but—apart from sounding rather pretentious—these tend to suggest a subcategory of work toward the top end of the skill scale. On the other hand, "information processor" falls into the opposite trap of suggesting that it applies only to the more routine work, like data entry. I notice that the European Commission's "New Ways to Work" unit has lately taken to talking about "e-work" and "e-workers." This is certainly in tune with the current fashion in New Labor Britain, where recent government statements on the "Information Age" policy include reference to the appointment of an "e-minister" to be in charge of "e-business" and an "e-envoy" to ensure that the policies are directed towards "e-inclusion." Perhaps "e-work" is indeed the least bad option.[1]

I was interested to receive the following reply from Alice de Wolff, a researcher based in Toronto:

I was amused by your discussion about what to call "it." We have had constant, very similar discussions about "the" term. Our experience is that there are two issues—one, to find an adequate description, and two, to find one that the workers involved relate to. We haven't managed to bring them together in any satisfactory way. When we use language other than "office workers" or "administrative professionals" (not my favorite), or "administrative assistants," the people who do the work don't think it's about them. I am most comfortable with "information workers," because I actually think it describes much of the work very well, and suggests a central location in the "information economy." I use it, and "front-line information workers," when I'm speaking with groups of office workers, and think it works well when used in context. But if we try to use it as a title of a document, event, etc., very few people relate.[2]

This encapsulates very well the tension that underlies any discussion of class: the tension between class as an analytical term (objective class position) and class as an aspect of personal identity (subjective class position). This in turn reflects the broader tension between structure and agency as conceptual frameworks for understanding the dynamics of social and economic change. I would not wish to minimize the difficulties of resolving these tensions in relation to other class categories, such as the "working class" or the "peasantry." Nevertheless the fact that such difficulties should arise so acutely in this context (which, for lack of a better term, I will call "office work" for the moment) is indicative of a particular lacuna in the history of socialist thought.

With a few notable exceptions, the literature on the subject leaves a distinct impression that on the whole socialists would rather not think about the subject at all, and when they have reluctantly had to do so, have been at a loss as to how to categorize office workers and whether to place them, with Crompton and Gallie, respectively, in a "white-collar proletariat" or "new working class"; to follow Lenin or Poulantzas in locating them as part of a petty bourgeoisie whose interests lie with small employers and are opposed to those of manual workers; or to hedge their bets along with Wright, and regard them as occupying "contradictory locations within class relations."[3] Marx supplies a modicum of support for each of these positions. In his account, the inevitable proletarianization of the petty bourgeoisie (craft and own-account workers and small employers) sits side by side with an equally inevitable expansion in the numbers of employed clerical workers (whom he terms "commercial wage workers"). However, he refuses the status of proletarian to the latter, stating that "the commercial worker produces no surplus value directly" because "the increase of this labor is always a result, never a cause of more surplus value." Furthermore, he is of the opinion that "the office is always infinitesimally small compared to the industrial workshop."[4]

This is not the place for a detailed overview of debates about class. It is worth noting, however, that some degree of muddle about where to locate office workers seems to persist whether class is defined in relation to occupation (which corresponds, as Marshall et al. have pointed out, with categories defined by the technical relations of production), to the social relations of production (the ownership or non-ownership of the means of production), to the social division of labor, to comparative income, to caste-based or other culturally constructed hierarchies (Weber's "status-groups") or to some empirically constructed stratification lacking any coherent conceptual underpinning, as in most official statistical categorizations.[5]

During the nineteenth century there were reasonable empirical grounds for regarding "clerks" as men. In the British Census of 1851, over 99 percent of people listed in this category were men. Despite an accelerating entry of women into the clerical workforce from the 1870s onward, most theorizing about the class position of office workers continued to be rooted in the assumption that they were masculine until the 1960s. The two classic studies of office workers in the postwar period, C. Wright Mill's *White Collar* and Lockwood's *The Black-Coated Worker* reveal this assumption only too clearly in their titles, which also, in their different ways, represent a sort of verbal throwing up of the hands in defeat at the problem of how to construct a conceptually coherent definition of office work.[6] If there is no other feature that uniquely delineates office workers from the rest of the workforce, we can feel these authors thinking, then at least they have their clothing in common.

Although one can sympathize with the label problem, such blindness is staggering. While these books were being written, women (clad, no doubt, in brightly-colored New Look shirtwaists or pastel twin-sweater sets) were entering office work in unprecedented numbers, so that by the time of the 1961 Census they represented about two-thirds of all clerical workers, in both Britain and the United States—a proportion that had risen to three-quarters by the 1971 Census. C. Wright Mills does in fact devote six pages of his 378-page opus to a discussion of the "white-collar girl" but characterizes her mainly in terms of her love life.[7] A discussion of gender plays no part in the formation of his bleak conclusion (essentially derived from Lenin) that white-collar workers will never develop distinctive forms of political agency and that even if they did, "their advance to increased stature in American society could not result in increased freedom and rationality. For white-collar people carry less rationality than illusion and less desire for freedom than the misery of modern anxieties."[8]

There is a blurred recognition in these authors' work that office workers cannot be regarded as a single homogenous entity. But this is combined with a strange reluctance to anatomize the differences within the broader category, which can seem on occasion like a willful refusal to see the obvious. This obliviousness offers a clue to the more general neglect of office work in socioeconomic analysis, and, more specifically, in socialist discourse. It confronts the analyst in a particularly acute form with the unresolved "woman question," which had been flapping about the attic of Marxist theory since its inception.

Most theories of class, at least until the 1960s, assigned women unproblematically to the class position of their fathers or husbands. If they were not economically dependent on these men, and played an independent role in the economy (something with which some theorists were already uncomfortable), then this did not pose major problems because they would normally occupy positions in the same class as these fathers or husbands—the wives and daughters of factory workers would also work in factories; the wives and daughters of rentiers would also be rentiers and so on (Marx's argument that domestic servants did not form part of the proletariat caused a few hiccups here, but not major ones, since servants were regarded as part of an obsolescent class and anyway merged into the reserve army of the lumpen proletariat from which there could be movement in and out of the proletariat without upsetting any important theoretical applecarts). In other words, arguments could be developed on the assumption that peoples' class positions *as citizens* (in which the basic unit is the household) were the same as their class positions *as workers* (in which the basic unit is the individual) and, indeed, that the former derived from the latter. While women are regarded simply as members of households, no tension between these different identities need arise and movements between classes (for instance by "marrying up" or "marrying down") can be dealt with under the heading "social mobility."

The minute female office workers are treated *as workers*, however, this simple mode of analysis breaks down. One is forced to confront the awkward fact that office workers may occupy a different class position from their husbands or fathers. The most thorough empirical study of class position in the United Kingdom of which I am aware concluded that "fully half of the conjugal units in our sample are cross-class families, using the three-category version of Goldthorpe's class schema."[9] Similar disparities arise using other classification methods, such as the Registrar General's categories used in U.K. official statistics, or Wright's neo-Marxist scheme.

This has implications not only for an analysis of the workforce but also for more general social analysis: if it is taken seriously, the household can no longer be perceived as a coherent political unit but must be recognized as fissured and complex; the atom must be split.

For the new generation of political analysts who came to adulthood in the 1960s and 1970s a serious examination of office work, *as work*, posed enormous theoretical challenges, which may be the most charitable explanation of why it was, comparatively speaking, so neglected as a subject among those who, at the time, were attempting to re-theorize class politics. There is, perhaps, another more personal reason, rooted in the class origins of this new generation of left intellectuals. In the United Kingdom, at least, the postwar welfare state opened up new forms of upward mobility for men and women of working-class origin. Selection at the age of eleven filtered a high-achieving minority into grammar schools from which they could enter the expanding university system. The novels and plays of the period are full of the class guilt that ensued. The act of leaving one's father's class was experienced acutely as an act of betrayal, but this was intertwined with an intoxication at the intellectual freedom of the new life of mental work. An oedipal delight at escaping from the authority of this father was combined with a romantic sense of loss and exile from the warmth and solidarity of the working-class community which was simultaneously both safe and claustrophobic, both politically revolutionary and morally oppressive. These were the upwardly mobile sons of the blue-collar heroes of Sennett and Cobb's *Hidden Injuries of Class*," the "brainy" (and by implication effete) students who sat indoors revising for their university entrance examinations while their sneering mates who had left school at fifteen flaunted their new leather jackets and motorbikes and spent their weekly wages on taking bouffant-haired girl-friends down to the Palais to rock and roll on a Friday night.[10] They felt both superior to and excluded from this new consumerist working-class culture and this, perhaps, inspired in them a permanent desire to earn the respect of these by-now-idealized working-class men. If they thought about women office workers at all, it was most usually as class accessories of the bourgeoisie. One archetype of the period is the secretary who acts as a gatekeeper for her boss. With her crisply accented "I'm sorry but he's in a meeting right now" and her unattainable sexual attractiveness, she can humiliate the working-class shop steward who is trying to gain access quite as effectively as the snootiest of head waiters. If any independent political agency is attributed to her at all, it is (perhaps with some unconscious projection) as a traitor to the working class.

Only some explanation like this, it seems to me, can make sense of the subsequent political development of this generation of male left intellectuals: the romanticization and stereotyping of specific forms of working-class life long after many of their features had already passed into history; the almost fetishistic preoccupation with certain types of male manual work (coal miners, autoworkers, truck drivers, dockers); the anxious and competitive display of their own working-class antecedents; the insistence that feminism was middle class and alienating to "real" working-class men.

In most cases it was not until the dawning of the 1980s that in their political imaginations they were able to accept that proletarian men were as likely to be picking up the kids from school while waiting for their wives to get home from the office as to be coming home grimy from the pit or factory expecting to find a meal on the table.

Perhaps because he had enough direct experience of manual work to have no need to prove his political virility in this respect, it was Harry Braverman who constituted the honorable exception to this pattern and undertook, in his monumental *Labor and Monopoly Capital,*" the first serious theoretical engagement with white-collar work that recognized the office as a differentiated locus of struggle between capital and labor.[11] He also demonstrated a link between technological change and change in the division of labor. His (essentially Marxist) "degradation" thesis was later challenged from a Weberian perspective by Goldthorpe, who argued that the empirical evidence (derived from a study of census data) did not support the proletarianization hypothesis but that, on the contrary, what was taking place was the development of a new "service class."[12] Perhaps more important than whether Braverman was "right" in the particulars of his analysis, this debate, coinciding as it did with a tremendous flowering of thoughtful feminist speculation about the relationship between class and gender, between paid and unpaid work, the nature of "skill," and the explanation for gender segregation in the labor market, opened up an immense and fertile field of inquiry.[13]

The resulting literature covered an enormous range: agit-prop handbooks designed to rouse office workers to action, like those by Tepperman and Gregory in the United States or Craig in Britain; serious academic studies, like those by Crompton and Jones in Britain or Game and Pringle in Australia; or more journalistic overviews giving anecdotal support to the proletarianization thesis, like those by Howe, Howard, or Siegel and Markoff, again in the United States.[14]

As well as raising a range of interesting questions, this added immeasurably to the store of empirical knowledge of the working conditions of office workers and the ways in which these were being transformed under the combined impact of the restructuring of markets, the ideological triumph of neoliberalism, and the impact of technological change. Most of these studies, however, reflect the fact that they took place within specific geographical locales. The labor markets they analyze are generally national or regional ones, and the workers' positions are mapped against those of their compatriots in other industries or occupations within these national labor markets. Although there have been a number of studies of globalization of blue-collar work, little account is taken of the implications of the relocation of non-manual work across national boundaries. A partial exception is a series of small-scale empirical studies of data entry workers in developing countries that implicitly follow Braverman's degradation thesis by drawing direct comparisons with the conditions of women workers in production work.[15] What is missing is an analysis that examines the position of these office workers both in their own local labor markets and in relation to their comparators in other countries.[16] This is an enormous task that I do not dare to attempt here. Instead, what I will try to do in the next section of this essay is to clear away some of the underbrush that is currently impeding clarity of thought in order to specify the sorts of questions researchers will need to address to produce the evidence that might render such an analysis possible in the future.

We begin by outlining some of the dimensions of the problem. Office workers (to stick, for the time being, with this unsatisfactory term) can be defined in at least six different ways: in terms of the *functional relationship of their work to capital*: in terms of their *occupations* (their place in the technical division of labor); their *social relation to production* (the ownership or non-ownership of the means of production); their place in the *social division of labor* (including the gender division of labor in the household); their *comparative income* (and hence their market position as consumers); and their social *"status."* Definitions constructed in these different ways are not necessarily coterminous and produce shifting and overlapping groups, riven with internal contradictions. And, of course, the structural categories thus created may not be recognized as relevant by the office workers themselves, who, in their upward or downward or horizontal trajectories across the boundaries between them may prefer to differentiate themselves by quite other criteria—their educational qualifications, for instance, or their consumption habits, or where they live, or, like Mills and Lockwood, the clothes they wear.

Any analysis is further complicated by the fact that the empirical data, in the form of official statistics, are constructed using classification systems that do not map neatly onto any of these analytical categories. Nevertheless, let us recapitulate the evidence, such as it is in relation to each of these approaches.

First, in terms of its *relation to capital*, office work can be regarded as covering the following functional categories: (a) design or elaboration of the content of products and services —including such things as software development, copyediting, the design of websites, product design, etc.; (b) purchase of inputs to these products or services and their sale—with an army of clerks whose numbers, according to Braverman, multiply exponentially as the number of transactions increases because of the need for the value of each transaction to be recorded by a "mirror" in a system that "assumes the possible dishonesty, disloyalty or laxity of every human agency which it employs"; (c) management of the production and distribution processes and of the workers themselves—descendants of the eighteenth-century "time keeper," this class now includes a range of human resources management and supervisory functions as well as logistical tasks; (d) circulation—much of the banking and financial services sector falls into this category, as do some accounting and retail functions; (e) reproduction of the workforce— activities associated with teaching, child care, health care, social work, etc.; (f) local, national, or international government functions connected with the provision of infrastructure, market management, and policing the population.[17]

Of these categories, only (c) and (d) correspond to Marx's "commercial workers," of whom he maintained, "The commercial worker produces no surplus value directly. . . the increase of this labor is always a result, never a cause of more surplus value."[18] Category (a) makes an input to the product in the form of knowledge in much the same way that a craft worker contributed skill in the past. Its existence as a separate non-manual task is merely a reflection of an increase in the division of labor. Workers in this category, it can be argued, contribute directly to the creation of surplus value insofar as the product of their labor is appropriated from them by the employer.

Such a typology could have been sketched out at any time in the last two hundred years. However, applying it in any specific case has been rendered immeasurably more complicated as the years have gone by, and the division of labor has grown more complex.

Perhaps the most important change that has taken place is the increasing commodification of "service" activities. In the comparatively simple markets that Marx and Engels observed it was feasible to regard the archetypal capitalist commodity as a physical object made in a factory designed either to be sold to another capitalist as a means to produce other physical objects (for instance, a loom, a vat, or a printing press) or to be sold to a wholesaler or retailer for final consumption by the consumer (a shirt, a bar of soap, or a newspaper). Since then, enormous elaborations have taken place. Each of the types of activity outlined above has itself become the basis of a host of new commodities, ranging from software packages to mind-controlling drugs, from electronic surveillance systems to credit cards, from educational CD-ROMs to baby alarms. Although the principles of economic analysis remain essentially the same, breaking their production down into their component parts and plotting their interactions with one another and with the fulfilment of the primary functions outlined above is an intricate and time-consuming business.[19] Indeed, in some cases the process can appear like zooming in on fractals, a descent into ever-smaller wheels within wheels as, with the seemingly inexhaustible inventiveness of capital, each area of human activity becomes the basis for profitable new commodities.[20] Within the production process of each commodity, even if it is carried out within a parent organization as a sort of sub-loop in the production process of another, the whole range of activities (design, management, execution, delivery to the customer) is reproduced in miniature. This task of assigning workers according to their functional relation to capital is rendered even more difficult by the increasingly complex division of labor within functions.

Analysis is complicated still further by changes that have taken place in the ownership structure of corporations. The combined effects of privatization, the disaggregation of large organizations into their component parts, convergence between sectors, cross-ownership, and "vertical integration" have made a nonsense of the tidy traditional divisions between "primary," "secondary," and "tertiary" sectors and between the "public" and "private" sectors of the economy, as well as between the subsectoral categories devised by government statisticians. The new "multimedia" sector, for instance, brings together organizations traditionally classified in many different places, including the public sector (state broadcasting corporations); metal-based manufacturing (computer hardware companies, via their software divisions and electronics manufacturers); printing and paper manufacture (publishers); record and tape manufacture; toy manufacture (the ancestors of some computer game companies); business and financial services (independent software companies that are not branches of computer manufacturers); film distributors; and telecommunications companies. Convergence is taking place in many other areas of the economy too; for instance, between banking and retailing and (thanks to biotechnology) between pharmaceuticals and agriculture.

Not only are the old sectors dissolving and new ones forming, but there are also complex interrelationships between the corporate actors involved. Some have entered into shifting alliances to carve up particular markets or to collaborate on the development of new products; others have bought stakes in each other (that is, in firms that the public imagine to be their competitors); and mergers, de-mergers, and takeovers are announced continuously.[21] To make matters even more complicated, in addition to these external realignments, most companies are also involved in a continuous process of internal reorganization, whereby individual functions are transformed into separate cost or profit centers, or floated off as separate companies. Add to this the impact of outsourcing to external companies and we arrive at a situation where corporations can no longer be regarded as stable and homogenous. Rather, they must be seen as mutually interpenetrating entities in constant flux, held together by an elaborate web of contracts in a continuous process of renegotiation. The sectorial classification of the "employer" to which any given worker is assigned is an almost accidental by-product of all these shenanigans, and this makes it impossible to use official statistics, at least in their present form, as a basis for serious analysis.

A second method of defining office workers is in relation to their *occupations*—the tasks that they carry out or their labor process. Where workers have been able to organize effectively in the past and set up professional associations or trade unions, and especially where negotiation has succeeded in making recognized qualifications a basis for limiting entry to particular trades or professions, these occupations can be said to be largely socially defined, their boundaries made explicit in these negotiations and their practices defined by custom and by the vigilance of the actors who stand to gain from the continuation of these forms of closure, to use Parkin's Weberian term.[22] In most cases, however, the tasks carried out by any given group of workers are determined in large part by the technical division of labor, and their labor processes are thus shaped by the design of the prevailing technology (which, it must be added, is itself shaped by the assumptions of those who commission it and in which the existing social relations of production are therefore already embedded).

Even in the occupational groups that have defended their inherited working practices most strongly against the assaults of the last quarter-century, it has been impossible to resist entirely the impact of information and communications technologies. Even doctors and lawyers, these days, not to mention telephone engineers, generally check their own e-mail from time to time, and the expectation of a personal secretary has all but disappeared among executives under the age of about forty-five, except for those who are very senior indeed. Meanwhile, across the rest of the workforce an extraordinary and unprecedented convergence has been taking place. From tele-sales staff to typesetters, from indexers to insurance underwriters, from librarians to ledger clerks, from planning inspectors to pattern-cutters, a large and increasing proportion of daily work time is spent identically: sitting with one hand poised over a keyboard and the other dancing back and forth from keys to mouse. Facing these workers on the screen, framed in pseudo bas relief, are ugly gray squares labeled, in whatever the local language, "File," "Edit," "View," "Tools," "Format," "Window," or "Help," the ghastly spoor of some aesthetically challenged Microsoft employee of the late 1980s. Gone are the linotype machine, the Rolodex, the card index, the sheaves of squared paper, the mimeograph, the drawing board, the cutting table, the telex machine, and all the other myriad tools of the mid-twentieth century, the mastery of which entitled one to a specific designation—the proud ownership of a unique skill. Gone too is the shared identity with other holders of that same skill. It must be remembered, of course, that the security bestowed by possessing these skills was often the security of the straitjacket. Limited transferability meant increasing vulnerability with each wave of technological innovation, but it did offer a basis for organizing, and playing some part in negotiating the terms on which the newer technology would be introduced.

The skills required to operate a computer and its various communications accessories should not, of course, be mistaken for the totality of the requirements of any given job. They are often ancillary to other "core" skills—the skills required to do "the job itself." However, these too may be undergoing a process of modification (which could take the form of routinization, or full commodification) that is changing their nature. Social workers, for instance, may find themselves filling out standard forms on-screen instead of writing or delivering in person more nuanced and qualitative professional reports on their clients; teachers may find themselves administering standard tests; insurance loss adjusters may have lost the discretion to decide what compensation a claimant should receive; Internet journalists may be required to write to tightly defined standard formats; and architects may be reduced to recombining standard components. Often these transformations are disguised by a change in the division of labor. The job description of a professional may be stripped down to its core and the numbers of such staff reduced, while the former components of the job that are capable of routinization are transferred to lower-skilled workers. Thus, for instance, routine inquiries to a computer help desk may be dealt with by the use of automated e-mail responses or by more junior staff, with only the really difficult problems routed through to the more highly paid "expert." Or sick people may be encouraged to call a call center staffed by nurses before making an appointment to see a doctor, as in the U.K. NHS Direct.

In general, it can be asserted that the number of tasks involving standard generic computer-related skills is growing rapidly, whether this is measured in terms of the numbers of people whose jobs involve these skills exclusively or in terms of the proportion of the time spent on these tasks by workers whose jobs also require other skills (or indeed both). This has curious and contradictory consequences. The fact that the skills are now generic has made it easier to skip laterally from job to job, company to company, and industry to industry. But by the same token each worker has also become more easily dispensable, more easily replaceable; thus the new opportunities also constitute new threats. The combination of this new occupational mobility with the huge expansion of the potential labor pool has also made it much more difficult to build stable group identities based on shared skills. Attempts to construct barriers around skill groups are thwarted by the speed of change. Any investment of time and effort in learning a new software package may be wiped out in a matter of months by the launch of a replacement. Existing hierarchies are challenged at precisely the moment that new fault lines are created. At the head office, e-mail brings senior and junior members of staff into direct communication with one another, cutting out middle layers of management, and a strange new camaraderie develops between colleagues of different grades as one shows the other how to eliminate a virus, or unzip an obstinate attachment. But simultaneously an unbridgeable gulf may have opened up between these same head office staff and their fellow employees at a remote call center, or data-processing site. When the only thing that can be predicted with certainty is that there will be more change, it is difficult to generalize broadly about occupational trends: while some processes are Taylorized and deskilled, others become more complex and multiskilled; while some groups are excluded, others find new opportunities opening up. An interesting empirical study recently completed in Canada by Lavoie and Pierre Therrien explored the relationship between computerization and employment structure. Following Wolff and Baumol, these researchers divided occupations into five categories: "knowledge workers," "management workers," "data workers," "service workers," and "goods workers" and concluded that the category in which there was the greatest growth associated with computerization was not, as popular mythology would have it, the "knowledge workers" but the "data workers"—those who "manipulate and use the information developed by the knowledge workers."[23] This provides some support for the argument that the trend towards routinization outweighs, in numerical terms, the tendency for work to become more creative, tacit, and multiskilled.

The official statistics contain no categories labeled "website designer" or "call center operator" or the other new occupational categories that are emerging, although these figure in job advertisements and are clearly operational in the labor market. The question is, how permanent are they likely to be? And will they form the basis of new collective identities? Or will workers choose to group themselves in relation to some other variable, such as the employer they work for, or the site where they are based? The answer to this question will be a crucial determinant of the extent to which new class identities will develop independently of geography, and of the potential for organizing at a transnational level.

A third approach to characterizing office workers involves analyzing their *relationship to the means of production*. Put crudely, in the classic Marxist formulation, if workers own the means of production, they are part of the bourgeoisie; if they are waged workers working for an employer who owns the means of production (and thereby produce surplus value), then they can be assigned to the proletariat. Self-employed workers and proprietors of small firms, in this model, belong to a petit bourgeoisie that will in due course be steadily squeezed out in the primary struggle between capital and labor, its members pauperized or proletarianized, except for a lucky few who become capitalists.

But this model too is becoming increasingly difficult to apply to office workers. First, the tendency of self-employment to die out has obstinately refused to take place. Although it has not expanded at the rate hoped for by neoliberals during the 1980s, self-employment remains fairly constant, at least in most developed countries. Across the European Union, for instance, the self-employed constituted a hardly varying 15 percent of the workforce over the two decades from 1975 to 1996.[24] This catch-all statistical category includes a range of different class positions. At one extreme are the self-employed with a few employees who can perhaps be regarded as petit bourgeois in the classic sense; then there are genuine freelancers, who work for a range of different employers; and at the other extreme are casual workers whose self-employed status is a reflection of labor market weakness—people who lack the negotiating muscle to insist on a proper employment contract even though they are effectively working for a single employer. Despite the lack of change in their overall numbers, the evidence from the United Kingdom suggests that the composition of this group is changing, in the direction of the casual end of the spectrum. A study by Campbell and Daley found that the proportion of self-employed people with employees fell from 39 percent to 31 percent between 1981 and 1991, while Meager and Moralee found that new entrants to self-employment were more likely than their earlier counterparts to be young, female, and entering relatively low-value-added service activities.[25] After analyzing data from the British Household Panel Survey, they concluded that the chances of a self-employed person being in the lowest earning category (the lowest 10 percent) were three times those of an employee. Even when an allowance was made for the underreporting of income by the self-employed, the chances were still twice as high.[26]

Self-employment is not necessarily a permanent state, however. Another study by Meager and Moralee, based on a longitudinal analysis of European Labor Force Survey data, uncovered high rates of inflow and outflow.[27] This makes it difficult to regard self-employment as a stable marker of class identity; for some it might merely be a staging post between different jobs.

Another factor that makes it difficult to regard the self-employed as a separate category is the increasing tendency to manage employees "as if" they are self-employed or, to use Rajan's phrase, to insist on "mind-set flexibility."[28] Practices such as management by results and performance-related pay, with contracts in which working hours are not specified, combine with intensified pressures of work and fear of redundancy to produce a situation in which the coercive power of the manager is internalized. The pace of work is therefore driven by a self-generated compulsive drive rather than the explicit authority of the boss. Closer to the piece-work rates of the putting-out systems than the time-based pay (albeit with machine-paced work) of the factory, this method of management muddles the relationship between worker and employer, a muddle that is intensified when there is also a physical separation between them. One worker in twenty in the British workforce, and a slightly higher proportion in North America, Scandinavia, and the Netherlands (though less in the rest of Europe) now works from home at least one day a week using a computer with a telecommunications link to deliver work. Of these, nearly half are formally self-employed. Since most of these workers own their own computers, it might be tempting to regard them as the twenty-first-century equivalent of home-based hand-loom weavers, but can stand-alone personal computers really be regarded as the means of production? A loom can be used to produce cloth quite independently of any other loom, whereas in most cases the value of the computer to the employer rests on its being linked to others, in a system that is not owned by the worker.

This is a moot point, which there is no space to investigate further here. It relates interestingly, however, to another question which has some pertinence. At least in a highly commodified economy, it is arguable that in order to make sense of individuals' general relation to capital (and hence their class position) it is necessary to consider not only their relation to the means of production but also to the "means of consumption" or "means of reproduction."[29]

The inexorable process of commodification has resulted in the decline of consumer service industries and their replacement by capital goods. In order to service themselves and their families, get themselves to work, and otherwise function it is increasingly necessary for workers to invest in such capital goods, from cars to washing machines. In addition, the only way to achieve a decent standard of housing is to purchase their own homes. The need to pay for all these goods locks workers ever more tightly into the market. As Andrew Carnegie was shrewd enough to notice over a century ago, a working class that owns its own housing is the best possible protection against strikes and uprisings.[30] It is then at least arguable that the degree to which they have succeeded in purchasing these things might affect workers' subjective view of their own class position. Whether it could be said to constitute an objective difference is a matter for investigation. There may be an analogy between workers' relationship to the "means of reproduction" and their relationship with the "means of production" according to which the homeowner occupies a position analogous to that of the independent craft worker, or proprietor of a one-man business. This analogy can be taken further: the division of labor in "reproduction work" does not necessarily just involve householders themselves. They may also employ cleaners, child-care workers, or other servants, thus occupying a place in the division of labor in reproduction work that is the equivalent of that of a small employer in production.[31] This issue is especially important in considering the class position of the "new" information workers in developing or newly developed countries, where the employment of servants, including live-in servants, is more common. In Hong Kong, for instance, Greenfield reports that it is usual for skilled manual workers, such as engineers, and lower-paid office workers, such as call center workers, direct sales workers, mobile and paging company workers, living in low-rent accommodations, to employ a live-in domestic "helper." "Working families whose incomes simply cannot accommodate a domestic helper still hire them, then exert extreme pressure on their helpers to minimize costs so that they can "get their money's worth." There is a even a growing tendency to hire "cheaper" Indonesian domestic helpers than Filipinas who number 350,000. It is interesting to note that in the aftermath of the Asian financial crisis the Hong Kong government intervened to alleviate the hardship of the average Hong Kong family by freezing the wages of domestic helpers."[32]

The use of non-occupational variables to assign workers to a class position is, to the best of my knowledge, untested and requires further analysis. It is particularly interesting in the context of the growth in homeworking, however, since the homeworker supplies many of the things more usually provided by the employer: the workspace, storage space, heating, lighting, insurance, setting-up and putting-away time, management and monitoring (in the form of self-management, filling in reports and time sheets, etc.) as well as incurring various risks to health and security. The home computer plays an interesting and ambiguous role in this, since it is an instrument both of production and of reproduction, as likely to be used for ordering the groceries or the kids' homework as for the work itself.

Information and communications technologies play a pivotal role in blurring the boundaries between work and consumption, constituting as they do a shifting interface between server and served. An order for an airline ticket, for instance, may be transmitted over the telephone and keyed in by a call center worker or entered directly onto the airline's website by the customer; the labor of data entry may be either paid or unpaid. It is therefore difficult to separate a discussion of the division of labor in paid "production" work from a more general discussion of the division of labor in unpaid, "consumption" work, which, highly gendered as it is, brings one to the more general discussion of the *social division of labor*, the fourth category in our list, but one that is beyond the scope of this essay to address in detail.

Our fifth category is the simple empirical one of *relative income*. For those wishing to model society as a tidy hierarchical pyramid, this has posed problems for over a century. The poor but genteel clerk who earns less than the vulgar navvy features in many nineteenth-century novels, from Dickens to Gissing, and survives well into the twentieth century, for instance, in Forster's *Howards End*, Grossmith's *Diary of a Nobody*, and some of Orwell's gloomier grubby-net-curtained novels. This clerk is presented as having traded money for a foothold (albeit precarious) in the middle classes and forms a male counterpart to the impoverished but well-educated governess hovering uneasily in an ambiguous social space between the servants' quarters and the drawing room (although his origins are likely to be humbler than hers, and his accent more suburban, his gender depriving him of the ever-latent potential for class elevation or downfall that constitutes the inherent inner drama of the feminine state).

The separation of status from income underlies most systems of class ranking, even the most empiricist and least theoretically grounded. It is explicit in the rationale for the Registrar General's Categories, which are used for class analysis in the British official statistics. A paper written in 1928 by a senior official at the General Register Office argued against classification by income, asserting that "any scheme of social classification should take account of culture. . . [which] the occupational basis of grading has a wholesome tendency to emphasize." In his opinion the criterion should be "the general standing within the community of the occupations concerned."[33]

Crompton and Jones note that there was parity between the earnings of male clerks and skilled manual workers from 1918 to 1936. For the next four decades, clerical workers' earnings declined in relative terms so that by 1978 they earned less than the average for all manual workers, with even the average wage for semi-skilled male manual workers exceeding that for male clerical workers. The earnings of female clerical workers were even lower, of course: rising from 42 percent of men's in 1913 to 57 percent in the mid-1950s and 74 percent by the end of the 1970s.[34] By the end of the 1990s, the hourly earnings of women clerical workers had reached 80 percent of men's across the European Union.[35] Clerical workers clearly fall below most manual workers in terms of their purchasing power.

Now that much information-processing work can be moved from region to region and country to country using electronic links, it becomes necessary to compare earnings between countries as well as within them. Such comparisons are difficult to make with precision because of variations in the structure of taxation and benefit systems, but in the form of "total labor costs" they figure prominently in the calculations made by employers when deciding what functions to locate where. And there are of course major differences. According to UNCTAD figures, in 1994 the average annual salary of a software programmer in India was $3,975, compared with $14,000 in Malaysia, $34,615 in Hong Kong, $31,247 in the United Kingdom, $45,552 in France, $46,600 in the United States, and $54,075 in Germany.[36] It is important, however, to be aware that such differences may be transient. The very success of the software industry in Bangalore, for instance, has resulted in a rapid inflation of local salaries that are now considerably higher than in other parts of India, such as Calcutta, where the supply of such skills still greatly exceeds demand, and in other parts of the world, for instance, Russia, where routine programming activities, such as coding, are now subcontracted from India. Khilnani describes the impact on the local labor of the large-scale influx of foreign multinationals into Bangalore: "These companies have transformed the wage structure of the Indian professional world. They are able to offer Indians in their late twenties salaries not even reached at the retirement points of Indian public enterprise salary scales."[37]

It is possible that such developments may signal the beginning of a global convergence in wages for workers with such specific and definable IT skills in activities that are capable of being carried out independently of location. Such a convergence, if it were taking place (and so far too little empirical research has been carried out to substantiate this) would imply a substantial gain for workers in developing countries combined with a reining in of real wage increases (if not an actual decline) in developed countries. That such increases would trickle down into the rest of the local economy in the developing countries cannot, however, be taken for granted. New forms of polarization might well develop between the holders of delocalizable jobs and workers whose jobs are geographically fixed. The extent to which the delocalizable jobs will take root in any given geographical spot is also dependent on a number of variables. If they take the form of labor-only subcontracting, then their anchoredness is highly contingent. There is always a choice open to the ultimate employer whether to send the jobs to the people or bring the people to the jobs, in the process known in the software industry as "body shopping." For at least two decades it has been a common practice for planeloads of software engineers to be flown from India to London, Frankfurt, Los Angeles, or other sites where their skills are needed. Typically, in the 1980s and early 1990s, they were employed by subcontractors. In 1992, liberalization of trade made it possible for the first time for software to be exported from sites in India, and a large-scale software export industry grew up based in Bangalore, and later in other centers such as Hyderabad, Poona, and Chennai. However, employers still retain a choice, and both the United States and most European countries have recently loosened their immigration procedures to make it easy to give green cards to software engineers with scarce skills. Where there is a global market for skills, the employer's choice whether or not to relocate is therefore mirrored by the worker's decision whether to migrate or stay put.

Not all the new delocalized work involves technical software skills. In many developing countries there has also been a major growth in lower-skilled clerical work, such as data entry and typing, and in call center work. Here the earnings may well compare unfavorably with those of well-organized production workers. Gothoskhar describes how "in the Indian context, the pay-levels of the younger call center workers may be much lower than those of middle-aged blue-collar workers." However, she goes on to point out that a comparison based only on income may be misleading in terms of defining their class position: "But the very criteria of recruitment of these workers as of today are such that they are from two-income families, mostly from 'white-collar' parents, people with an education in English, and so on. This today at least excludes people from lower castes, people from the rural areas, people whose parents are from what may be called the 'traditional working class' families."[38]

This brings us to the sixth category, a class definition based in a notion of *status*. This term, in its Weberian sense, can be extended to cover a range of different variables including ethnicity, language group, religion, skin color or caste, or even the condition of slavery. The structure of most labor markets (and the history of most labor movements) bears powerful testimony to the force of such differences in creating patterns of inclusion and exclusion, privilege and deprivation. Labor markets are segmented along racial lines in North America, Europe, Australia, and Japan quite as much (if sometimes more covertly) as they are in many developing countries. However, the fault lines may fall somewhat differently. One important factor is language. Entry to the new world of information work is crucially dependent on the ability to understand, speak, and write English, or, in some parts of the world, French, Spanish, German, Japanese, or Arabic. In countries where this is not the native language, this is likely to be the prerogative of the highly educated. Immediately, the threshold is raised above that required in the imperial parent economy. Differences in the supply of and demand for labor and relative wage levels also play their part, of course. It is therefore not unusual to find the sorts of work that are carried out by school-leavers, or graduates from junior college in the United States being carried out by graduates or postgraduates in a developing country. Sinclair Jones studied a medical transcription center in Bangalore carrying out work for doctors in the United States. She reports that in the United States the work was done by homeworkers, paid a piece-rate for the number of lines time, who would normally be educated only to community college level, but that applicants in India generally arrive with a master's degree. Nevertheless, "Even though there is a rather paradoxical disparity between the qualifications base of the U.S. and Indian workers there are still huge cost advantages to undertaking this work in India. For graduates in India with, for example, a Master of Arts, there are limited options for employment. As an English teacher in Bangalore they might earn around Rupees 3000 per month [approx. U.S. $75]." However, in the transcription center, "a good transcriptionist with two years experience earns between Rupees 7,500 and 9,500 per month [U.S. $190–$240] whilst some are earning over Rupees 12,000 [U.S. $300] per month. This compares with workers in the U.S. who earn between $1,800 and 2,400 a month. The experienced Indian medical transcriptionist is then about eight times cheaper than a U.S. counterpart."[39] Her social status in the local economy will nevertheless be quite different.

This has implications for how office workers identify their own interests and their potential for making common cause with other workers doing identical work in other countries. This question is complicated by another issue. Where workers are employed by foreign companies, the exploitation of labor by capital may not be perceived as such but rather as an imperial exploitation of natives by colonialists.[40] Instead of perceiving their interests as being aligned with those of other workers employed by the same multinational companies, they may perceive their interests as national ones, best served by aligning themselves with local capitalists against the imperializing outsiders. Such attitudes are likely to be reinforced by any encounters with racist attitudes among the workers of the developed world.

We must conclude that although there is considerable potential for the emergence of a common class consciousness among information-processing workers based in a common labor process, common employers, and a common relation to capital, powerful counterforces are present that seem likely to inhibit this development, the greatest of which, perhaps, is racism.

There is considerable evidence of successful organizing by the new "e-workers" within countries, as indicated by the 1999 strike by call center workers at British Telecom in the United Kingdom and unionization among data entry workers in the Caribbean and in Brazil.[41] There is also some evidence that employers consciously avoid areas where workers are likely to organize when selecting locations. In her study of the medical transcription center in Bangalore, Sinclair Jones reports, "The informant did comment that in the early stages they had considered establishment in Kerala on the basis that it has extremely high literacy levels. However, Kerala also has high levels of industrial organization and the company decided not to take the risk. This kind of service provision is extremely vulnerable to stoppages given the commitment to rapid turn around and the company management actively seeks to avoid becoming exposed to attempts at organizing labor."[42]

However, examples of such organization across national boundaries are few and far between. One notable exception is the agreement covering call center workers jointly signed with Air Canada by the Canadian Auto Workers Union and their sister unions in the United Kingdom and the United States. In general, the evidence of resistance by these workers comes in more sporadic and anarchic forms, such as the writing of viruses or other forms of sabotage.

One factor that will undoubtedly influence the propensity of workers to organize and take militant action will be the extent to which this is likely to be in their own economic best interests. If low-level office work is perceived as the bottom rung of a ladder that can be scaled successfully by keeping on the right side of the boss, then hard work, keeping one's nose clean, and sycophancy will offer the best route to advancement. If, on the other hand, no promotion prospects seem likely—for instance, because the higher levels are located on another site halfway across the globe, or because only men, or only white people, or only people with of a certain nationality or caste ever get promoted—then the best way to better one's income may well seem to lie with making common cause with one's fellow workers. Once again, we find that gender and race play a crucial role in determining class identity.

It is apparent that a new cybertariat is in the making. Whether it will perceive itself as such is another matter.

/ 11 / WHO'S WAITING?: THE CONTESTATION OF TIME

THE CONCEPT OF TIME SOVEREIGNTY PLAYS A CRUCIAL ROLE in most notions of what constitutes the quality of life. Studies of working life have shown that autonomy and control over the work progress make a critical contribution to a sense of well-being and job satisfaction, while their lack is a major contributor to stress-related disorders.

Negotiations between employers and workers have, over the centuries, centered on time: the imposition of "clock time" over the more leisurely and varied rhythms of the preindustrial age; set-piece battles over the length of the working day or week, or the granting of holidays; and continuing conflicts over the speed of work, with successive waves of technology giving employers more and more precision in their control over the pace of work, while also giving workers ever more ingenious means of resisting.

This pattern of contested ownership of time does not stop at the factory gate.

In feminist and other readings it continues in different forms in the household and the broader community. Comparative studies of the disproportionate amounts of time spent on various household and care tasks are regarded as clinching evidence for the continuing social oppression of women who are presented in some accounts as being in continual struggle with men over who does what in the household. Phrases such as "free time" or "time to myself" have come to act as stand-ins for leisure and pleasure.

The time that is at issue in these contests has a dual aspect: a quantitative one—the *amount* of time conceded to the other party; and a qualitative one—the *control* of that time by its subject.

Whether it is donated freely in a loving relationship, appropriated coercively in a less loving one, or exchanged for money, time in this dual sense is perhaps the most basic human asset. Except in exceptional cases (for instance, the possession of large amounts of inherited or accumulated capital) in combination with whatever skills we have and diligence to apply them, our time is ultimately all that we human beings have to trade in the multidimensional market we call "society." And our success in negotiating on both these fronts—qualitative and quantitative—arguably makes a greater contribution to the quality of our lives than any other single factor, always assuming, of course, that the basic means of subsistence are available.

It is the contention of this chapter that the conflicts between employers and workers over time are deeply and dynamically connected with other social conflicts over time, and that they therefore have an impact, not just on the quality of working life but also over the general quality of life of all citizens, regardless of whether they are in employment or not.

Let me repeat an argument I have made throughout this book: It is possible to view economic history as a history of progressive commodification. By this I mean the slow transformation of activities carried out for simple use or for exchange outside the money economy into activities carried out for monetary gain. Typically, an activity that begins as an unpaid domestic activity (for example, washing clothes) becomes the basis of a service activity (a laundry service), which in turn, with the assistance of technological advances, becomes the basis for new manufacturing industries (making washing machines, tumble dryers, detergent, or fabric conditioners).

These three spheres (unpaid labor, service provision, and manufacture) interact dynamically with one another. For instance, the time spent on the unpaid labor of washing clothes does not simply evaporate to be made available for "leisure"; it is transformed into new forms of unpaid labor: in the first stage labeling, listing, checking, and sorting the items to be washed and negotiating with the laundry; in an intermediate stage, perhaps, going to a communal public laundry or Laundromat; in a later stage, purchasing the new chemical products and machines, grasping and following the instructions for using them, and carrying out the associated activities that are still imperfectly automated, such as sorting, ironing, folding, storing, or sewing on replacement buttons. The manufacturing industries in turn give rise to new service activities: new product development, design, marketing, distribution, maintenance, and, as products become ever more complex, the provision of technical information to customers on how to operate the products.

The inexorable drive toward the creation of more and more "products" is therefore closely associated on the one hand with the creation of new forms of "consumption work" and on the other with a growth in "service work."

Needless to say, all of these activities take time to execute. In some cases the "time" can be said to have been converted from unpaid time to paid time or *vice versa*. In other cases the time may remain paid or unpaid, but the changes in skill requirements and labor processes may have led to dramatic changes in the degree of autonomy exercised by the individuals involved, whether in their capacities as paid workers or unpaid consumption workers.

The process of commodification is not limited to the production of the sorts of goods that can be purchased from shops or showrooms, ever-burgeoning though these are. It also extends across the service sector and into all other areas of the economy, including those that have traditionally been regarded as "public goods." A number of interlinked processes are currently contributing to this state of affairs.

One of these is the application of new technologically enabled systems to areas of bureaucratic life that were formerly resistant to being standardized and routinized. Increasingly, the use of individual professional judgment in decision making is being overridden by "intelligent" systems which substitute a series of standard rules; for example, to determine eligibility for a bank loan or mortgage, prioritization for hospital treatment, or the offer of a university place to an applicant. As soon as the labor involved in processing such decisions has been standardized, it becomes possible to quantify its outputs, turn the function into a separate profit center or cost center, externalize it, or open it up to competitive tender.

A second related factor has been the increasingly generic nature of many business functions and processes resulting from a remarkable convergence of technologies, and hence of labor processes, and the monopolistic dominance of global markets by a few standard suppliers, notably Microsoft. It should be noted in this context that the design of "off the peg" software increasingly dictates the nature of business procedures, forcing many small firms, for instance, to use standard procedures for project management, accounting, or database design because they lack the intellectual, technical, and financial resources to create their own "bespoke" solutions in an increasingly complex technological environment. As organizations develop their business processes in these near-interchangeable ways, it becomes easier and easier for these same processes to be seen not, as in the past, as internal "overheads" or "head office services" but as separable functions, capable of being outsourced, "in-sourced," or indeed sold on as profit-making services to other organizations.

A third factor has been the increasing *telemediation* of service delivery. This in turn has resulted from a combination of factors, including the falling cost and rapid spread of cheap telecommunications and computing technologies, the globalization of markets, and the growth of a twenty-four-hour culture. This growth has been characterized by a self-affirming pattern whereby service workers are increasingly obliged to access other services outside "normal" hours in their capacities as consumers, thus creating a need for still more service workers to be available to supply them in a vicious circle that has already eroded many traditional temporal boundaries. The growth of telemediated service delivery has led to a boom in call centers and the increasing adoption of a call center model for a vast range of services across virtually all sectors of the economy, including the public sector.

A fourth contributory factor has been the privatization, liberalization, or opening up to competition of public services, ranging from the cleaning of hospitals to the management of residential homes, from the delivery of letters to the processing of tax claims.

Even when services remain in public ownership, requirements that they should compete with private services place a new emphasis on the close monitoring of processes (often linked to requirements to meet "targets") and costs, and the avoidance of "inefficiencies." As Jean Gadrey, among others, has pointed out, such "inefficiencies" may consist precisely of those tasks (such as chatting to a lonely elderly customer over a post office counter), which in the past have brought meaning and motivation to the lives of public service workers, and satisfaction to their clients.

The logic of commodification extends beyond those areas of human activity that have already been transformed into products or services that are already sold on the market. It also leads to a mind-set in which other types of activity are treated "as if" they are commodities even when they are still being offered for their intrinsic use value. Local government bodies, for instance, may become acutely aware of the market value of land currently being used for social purposes, such as school sports grounds, or of buildings being used to house the sick or the disabled, or ask themselves what "value for money" is being gained from a bereavement counseling service or a library.

We thus have a situation where large swathes of the workforce have had their roles transformed. Instead of delivering use values and, in Weberian terms, being motivated by a care ethic, they are providing standard products or services for economic exchange and are more likely to be motivated by simple economic instrumentality.

Whether it is being done in the name of profitability, increasing speed of delivery or market share, efficiency, or "giving the taxpayer value for money," the focus is increasingly on the financial bottom line—avoiding waste and keeping costs to a minimum.

In most service industries the main costs are labor costs. This creates an enormous pressure on managers to find ways to reduce them. There are a number of ways to achieve this, many of which lend themselves to concurrent adoption. One method is to move to a region where labor costs are lower, an option which is increasingly adopted for telemediated functions that involve no face-to-face contact with clients and employ generic skills and knowledge that can already be found in a number of places or acquired fairly quickly and easily. Another method is to routinize as many tasks as possible and delegate them to low-skilled, low-waged staff, leaving the more highly paid specialists only those tasks they alone can fulfill. A variant on this strategy involves making explicit and codifying as much as possible the knowledge of these specialists and embedding it in software, systems, or tools that can be accessed easily by nonspecialists, such as interrogable websites. Finally, labor can be externalized, so that the unpaid time of the service consumer is substituted for the paid time of the service worker.

The externalization of labor as a cost-saving strategy is not new. In the 1950s, the self-service concept was introduced to shops, leading to the development of the supermarket. In the 1960s, it began to be introduced in the banking sector, starting with the simple expedient of persuading customers to fill in their own deposit slips, and continuing until, with the development of the ATM, the paid labor of bank tellers could be replaced almost entirely by the unpaid labor of bank customers. Since then, often under the guise of improving the user experience by reducing waiting time, the self-service principle has been introduced across a wide range of sectors.

In its first stages, this externalization is often welcomed by consumers, who feel empowered by it. Faced with waiting in a long line to buy a railway ticket, investigate the availability of a library book, fill a car with gas, or have the vegetables weighed and labeled, most people prefer to do it themselves, even if this means grappling with an unfamiliar user interface. Problems start arising when there is no longer a choice; when the alternative of being served by a human being has been eliminated and the individual is left to encounter the ATM machine, the self-service ticket machine, or the unattended gas pump alone. Then, if the machine is malfunctioning in some way, or if one lacks some of the skills or abilities to access it (for instance, if one is partially sighted or in a foreign country) or if one's needs are unusual and not catered for by the standard menu of options, the consumer is left helpless. Not only are the consumer's needs left unsatisfied, it is likely that many hours of (unpaid time) may be used up as a result. The device that was originally meant to save time has ended up wasting it. Once the human alternative has been eliminated, there is no incentive for providers to ensure an adequate supply of the machines unless there is on-the-spot competition from an alternative supplier, and customers may find themselves once again waiting in long lines, though this time to be served by a machine rather than a human being.

With the introduction of telemediation an extra dimension is added. Regardless of the location of the service workers, as their workload expands and costs escalate, managers look for ways to maximize their productivity. One way to do this is to encourage the customer to do as much work as possible—for instance, by selecting routing options from automated menu systems and keying in their own membership numbers and other information. The user interface is not with a physical machine in "real" space (though many machines may be involved) but involves a "virtual" encounter over distance by telephone. Instead of waiting in a "real" line, where at least one can talk to fellow waiters, one is increasingly held in a "virtual" line. And, as waiting times in telephone queues are lengthened, incentives are created for customers to go one further and cut out the human operator altogether by serving themselves via the Internet. Indeed, so profitable is it for service providers to have their customers do this that they often offer lower prices for self-service customers.

Allied to this externalization of labor are various other practices designed to increase the efficiency and reduce the costs of service delivery. More and more sophisticated routing of calls ensures that the most routine inquiries are dealt with by the most junior staff, with various filters ensuring that the most highly skilled professionals only deal with complex problems. Staff are tightly monitored, with prewritten scripts designed to make sure that they get through each call as quickly as possible while payment systems are designed to reward high productivity.

These developments have an impact not only on the quality of working life for service workers but also on the quality of nonworking life (or at least nonpaid work) for service users.

It is important not to romanticize the quality of the user experience in the past. Bureaucratized forms of service delivery have often been associated with delays and frustrations, especially during periods of economic shortages, or under conditions of centralized bureaucratic control. One has only to read Kafka or accounts of shopping in pre-1989 Russia to be aware that for many consumers, the chance to "let one's fingers do the walking" and order by telephone can be a profoundly liberating experience. Indeed, there are very few people who could put their hands on their hearts and say that they would unequivocally welcome a return to a world in which all encounters are face-to-face.

Nevertheless, it must be acknowledged that the present wave of labor externalization, particularly where this is telemediated, has profound impacts, some of which may not be so positive.

At the most obvious level, a world in which access to more and more services is by means of telephone or the Internet and human face-to-face counterparts are increasingly rationed, charged for at premium rates, or eliminated altogether presents major issues of exclusion for people without access to the infrastructure, hardware, or software; for people who lack the language, literacy, or social skills to use them effectively; and for people whose eyesight, hearing, or mental or manual dexterity is impaired in such a manner as to make their use difficult or impossible.

There is, however, a more general level at which everyone is affected. The pressure on service delivery workers to minimize transaction time creates a production-line approach and emphasizes quantitative targets. The service delivery agency's interests lie in ensuring that all staff are fully productive at all times. This implies a "just-in-time" rather than a "just-in-case" level of staffing since the latter would involve having some staff idle during slack periods. This means that queuing at a busy time is almost inevitable, but it is the customer's, rather than the worker's time that is wasted in the waiting process. The same process that creates stress for the worker therefore also causes frustration in the customer.

Furthermore, the service delivery agency's interests also imply a minimization of transaction time. Having waited for some time in a virtual line, customers often wish to express themselves freely. However, this is actively discouraged by the tight scripting of the service worker's response. This sets up a further conflict of interest between worker and customer, a conflict often played out in a struggle for control of the agenda of the interchange—a struggle for control of time.

Let us say that a customer has been delivered the wrong product and rings up to the customer service department of a company to complain. Having dutifully worked her way through a series of menus and pressed the required keys she has been placed in a queue where, between bursts of recorded music, she is informed, "Your call is valuable to us. Please hold." After a considerable wait, the customer, by now feeling doubly aggrieved, is all ready to say, "Now look here, your company has made a mistake. I have paid you a lot of money for something I haven't received and I want something done about it." She wants, literally, to be "waited on." But when she finally reaches the front of the line, instead of being able to give vent to this justified annoyance, she is immediately cut off with a series of scripted requests for information. What is her address and zip code? What is her order reference number? What is the serial number of the product? Could she confirm her name? And the date on which she made the purchase? Any slight deviation from the norm (for instance, a difference between the address on her credit card and the delivery address) puts her into a special category that requires being put into another queue to await the attention of another stressed-out operator who requires a repetition of all this information. Any attempt to short-circuit this process and explain the problem in her own words produces a response (also carefully scripted) designed to make her sympathize with the plight of the poor service delivery worker— who is only, after all, doing his job—and to feel guilty for expressing the slightest annoyance. Both worker and customer are trapped in a situation beyond either's control, and unpleasant for both. Instead of embarking on a joint effort to solve a problem, they are pitted against each other. Many of the inhibitions against rudeness that come into play in a face-to-face situation are absent when dealing with a faceless, distant stranger. And the pressure on the service worker to meet productivity targets forbids the kind of social chat that can transform a chore into a pleasure when people meet across a counter or in a waiting room.

What is at issue here is time in both its quantitative and qualitative dimensions. Quantitative considerations include the amount of paid time "spent" by the worker, the amount "received" by the customer, in the form of personal attention, set against the time "spent" by the customer in waiting and responding to the service provider's scripted questions. Qualitatively, we must look at the degree of autonomy that can be exercised by the worker or the customer, and the extent to which the Taylorization of the labor process of the service worker, in combination with the externalization process, results inevitably in a parallel Taylorization of the consumption process.

Few empirical studies have been carried out of these processes and it is still a matter of conjecture what proportion of "leisure" time is spent in the consumption of commodified services by the average citizen, the extent to which this involves absorbing the externalized labor of service workers, the extent to which unpaid consumption work processes can be said to be affected by this form of Taylorization, or the rate at which these things are increasing. If, as seems likely, they are substantial, then there is a real danger that the apparently liberating information and communications technologies that have so increased both the range of services that can be accessed remotely and the distances over which they can be accessed may be leading to a degradation of the quality of daily life.

These developments open up a number of major questions not just for the development of frameworks for future empirical research, but for our very conception of society: What models of individual autonomy and choice can we use to understand human agency in an increasingly commodified economy? How should we conceptualize the increasingly fluid boundaries between "work" and "leisure," "production" and "consumption," "service delivery" and "service use"? When citizens are pitted against one another in their capacities as workers and as consumers, what forms of social organization are possible to enable them to express their collective interests and gain some purchase on their decision-making process? When both employment and consumption relationships are increasingly transacted over geographical distances, often across national borders, what forms of representation, negotiation, and regulation are possible?

NOTES

CHAPTER 1

1. Harry Braverman, *Labor and Monopoly Capital: The Degradation of Work in the Twentieth Century* (New York: Monthly Review Press, 1974).
2. Alice Clark, *Working Life of Women in the Seventeenth Century* (New York: A. M. Kelley, 1968).
3. Ann Oakley, *Woman's Work: The Housewife, Past and Present* (New York: Vintage Books, 1976).
4. Colin Tudge, *The Famine Business* (London: Faber & Faber, 1977).
5. Barbara Ehrenreich and Deirdre English, "The Manufacture of Housework," *Socialist Revolution,* October-December 1975.
6. Office for National Statistics, *Social Trends* (London: Office for National Statistics, 1977).
7. Office for National Statistics, *Family Expenditure Survey* (London: Office for National Statistics, 1976). See http://www.statistics.gov.uk/ssd/Surveys_family_expenditure_survey.asp.
8. Data from *Department of Employment Gazette,* November 1978.
9. I. Ann Barron and Ray Currow, *The Future with Microelectronics* (London: Frances Pinter, 1979).
10. Both quotes are from Rachael Grossman, "Silicon's Ugly Secrets," *Computing Europe,* 10 June 1979.

CHAPTER 2

1. Barbara Ehrenreich and Deirdre English, "The Manufacture of Housework," *Socialist Revolution,* October–December 1975.
2. Batya Weinbaum and Amy Bridges, "The Other Side of the Paycheck," *Monthly Review,* July–August 1976.

3. Jonathan Gershuny, *After Industrial Society?: The Emerging Self-Service Economy* (Atlantic Heights, N.J.: Humanities Press, 1978).

CHAPTER 3

1. Carnegie's views are discussed in Barbara Ehrenreich and Deirdre English, *For Her Own Good: 150 Years of the Experts' Advice to Women* (London: Pluto Press, 1979).
2. Jonathan Gershuny, *After Industrial Society?: The Emerging Self-Service Economy* (Atlantic Heights, N.J.: Humanities Press, 1978).
3. Batya Weinbaum and Amy Bridges, "The Other Side of the Paycheck," *Monthly Review,* July-August 1976.
4. This statistic is taken from the United Kingdom's Office for National Statistics, *New Earnings Survey* for the years 1980-1983. This survey is available now online at http://www.statistics.gov.uk.
5. For a more detailed discussion of the effects of new technology on women's employment, see Ursula Huws, *Your Job in the Eighties* (London: Pluto Press, 1982).
6. This experiment is described in detail by Tarja Cronberg and Inga-Lise Sangregorio, "More of the Same: The Impact of Information Technology on Domestic Life in Japan," *Development Dialogue* 2 (1981).
7. See Ursula Huws, "The Runaway Office Jobs," *International Labour Reports,* No. 2 (1984).
8. Described by Richard Clavaud, "Le Teletravail," *Telesoft,* no. 1 (December 1981–January 1982).

CHAPTER 4

1. See S. Brusco, "Labor Market Structures, Company Policies and Technological Progress: The Case of Italy," in *Capital and Labor,* ed. O. Diettrich and J. Morley (Brussels: EEC, 1981); L. Siegel et. al., *Background Report on Silicon Valley* (Mountain View, Calif.: Pacific Studies Center, 1982); B. Bluestone and B. Harrison, *The Deindustrialization of America* (New York: Basic Books, 1982).
2. M. Aldrich, *Videotext: Key to the Wired City* (London: Quiller Press, 1982).
3. Ursula Huws, *Your Job in the Eighties* (London: Pluto Press, 1982).
4. E. Appelbaum, *The Impact of Technology on Skill Requirements and Occupational Structure in the Insurance Industry* (Philadelphia: Temple University Press, 1984).
5. Ursula Huws, *The New Homeworkers: New Technology and the Changing Location of Whitecollar Work* (London: Low Pay Unit, 1984).
6. Ursula Huws, "The Runaway Office Jobs," *International Labour Reports,* no. 2 (March-April 1984).

CHAPTER 5

1. Alice Clark, *Working Life of Women in the Seventeenth Century* (New York: A. M. Kelley, (1968).
2. Ibid.
3. Jonathan Gershuny, *After Industrial Society?: The Emerging Self-Service Economy* (Atlantic Heights, N.J.: Humanities Press, 1978).
4. See Harry Braverman, *Labor and Monopoly Capital: The Degradation of Work in the Twentieth Century* (New York: Monthly Review Press, 1974).
5. Cynthia Cockburn, *Brothers* (London: Pluto Press, 1983).

CHAPTER 6

1. See Jeanne Mager Stellman, *Women's Work Women's Health: Myths and Realities* (New York: Pantheon, 1977).
2. See Wendy Chavkin, ed., *Double Exposure: Women's Health Hazards on the Job and at Home* (New York: Monthly Review Press, 1983).
3. For more on the working conditions of office workers, see Marianne Craig, *The Office Worker's Survival Handbook* (London: Women's Press, 1991) and Ursula Huws, The VDU *Hazard's Handbook* (London: Hazards Centre, 1987).
4. See Rosemary Pringle, *Secretaries Talk: Sexuality, Power, and Work* (London: Verso, 1989).

CHAPTER 7

1. See, among others, Ursula Huws, *The New Homeworkers: New Technology and the Relocation of White-Collar Work* (London: Low Pay Unit, 1984); "Remote Possibilities: Some Difficulties in the Analysis and Quantification of Telework," in *Telework: Present Situation and Future Development of a New Form of Work,* ed. W. B. Korte, S. Robinson, and W. J. Steinle (New York: Elsevier Science Publishers, 1988); and "Uprooting the Office," *Practical Computing,* September 1989.
2. J. C. Jones, "Automation and Design (1-5)," *Design* 103, 104, 106, 108, 110 (1957-1958).
3. See J. Nilles et. al., *The Telecommunications-Transportation Trade-off* (New York: John Wiley, 1976); R. C. Harkness, *Technological Assessment of Telecommunications-Transportation Interactions* (Menlo Park, Calif.: Stanford Research Institute, 1977).
4. See Daniel Bell, *The Coming of Post-Industrial Society* (New York: Basic Books, 1973): I. D. Illich, *Tools for Conviviality* (New York: Harper & Row, 1973); Charles A. Reich, *The Greening of America* (New York: Random House, 1970); and E. F. Schumacher, *Small Is Beautiful* (New York: Harper & Row, 1973).
5. Alvin Toffler, *The Third Wave* (New York: Bantam Books, 1981).
6. See Harry Braverman, *Labor and Monopoly Capital: The Degradation of Work*

in the Twentieth Century (New York: Monthly Review Press, 1974); 9 to 5, *Race Against Time: Automation of the Office* (Boston: National Association of Office Workers, 1980); and J. Barker and H. Downing, "Word Processing and the Transformation of the Patriarchal Relations of Control in the Office," *Capital and Class* 10 (1980).

7. Betty Friedan, *The Feminine Mystique* (New York: Dell Publishing, 1963).

8. See L. Comer, *Wedlocked Women* (Leeds, England: Feminist Books, 1974) and Ann Oakley, *Woman's Work: The Housewife, Past and Present* (New York: Vintage Books, 1976).

9. See S. Williams, *Politics Is for People* (Cambridge: Harvard University Press, 1981).

10. See M. Aldrich, *Videotext: Key to the Wired City* (London: Quiller Press, 1982).

11. See M. H. Olson, *Remote Office Work: Implications for Individuals and Organizations* (New York: New York University School of Business Administration, 1981); J. H. Pratt, "Home Teleworking: A Study of Its Pioneers," *Technological Forecasting and Social Change* 25 (2000); S. S. Kawakami, *Electronic Homework: Problems and Prospects from a Human Resources Perspective* (Urbana-Champaign, Ill.: Institute of Labor and Industrial Relations, 1983); Huws, *The New Homeworkers;* G. Vedel, *Just Pick Up a Telephone!: Remote Office Work* in *Sweden* (Copenhagen, Denmark: Copenhagen School of Economics and Business Administration, 1984); and M. Lie, *Is Remote Work the Way to the Good Life for Women as Well as Men?* (Trondheim, Norway: Institute for Social Research in Industry, 1985).

12. See L. Bisset and U. Huws, *Sweated Labour: Homeworking* in *Britain Today* (London: Low Pay Unit, 1984).

13. See B. A. Gutek, "Women's Work in the Office in the Future," in *The Technological Woman: Interfacing with Tomorrow,* ed. J. Zimmerman (New York: Praeger, 1983).

14. See U.S. Congress Office of Technological Assessment, *Automation of America's Offices* (Washington, D.C.: U.S. Government Printing Office, 1985); European Foundation for the Improvement of Living and Working Conditions, *Telework: Impact on Living and Working Conditions* (Dublin: European Foundation for the Improvement of Living and Working Conditions, 1984); National Research Council, *Office Workstations in the Home* (Washington, D.C.: National Academy Press, 1985); and Housing Associations Charitable Trust, *Planning for Homework* (London: Housing Associations Charitable Trust, 1984).

15. See J. Atkinson, *Flexibility, Uncertainty and Manpower Management* (London: Institute of Manpower Studies, 1984) and C. Curson, ed., *Flexible Patterns of Work* (Wellington, N.Z.: Institute of Personnel Management, 1986).

16. Jones, "Automation and Design (1-5)."

17. See U. Huws, J. Hurstfield, and R. Holtmaat, *What Price Flexibility? The Casualisation of Women's Employment* (London: Low Pay Unit, 1989).

18. See P. Judkins, D. West, and J. Drew, *Networking in Organisations. The Rank Xerox Experiment* (Hampshire, England: Gower Publishing, Ltd., 1985).

19. See Huws, "Remote Possibilities."

20. See Huws, "Uprooting the Office."

21. Tom Forester, "The Myth of the Electronic Cottage," *Futures* (June 1988).

CHAPTER 8

1. S. Rowbottom, *Women's Liberation and the New Politics* (Mayday Manifesto, 1969, reprinted Nottingham, England: Bertrand Russell Peace Foundation, 1971); *Women's Consciousness, Man's World* (London: Allen Lane, 1973); *Hidden from History* (London: Pluto Press, 1973).

2. J. Gardiner et. al., "Women's Domestic Labor," *New Left Review,* no. 89 (1975).

3. P. Freire, *Pedagogy of the Oppressed* (New York: Seabury Press, 1970).

4. Harry Braverman, *Labor and Monopoly Capital: The Degradation of Work in the Twentieth Century* (New York: Monthly Review Press, 1974).

5. J. Barker and H. Downing, "Word Process and the Transformation of Patriarchal Relations," *Capital and Class* 10 (1980).

6. See Chapters 1 and 2 above; also, "Consuming Fashions," *New Statesman & Society* (1988).

7. Conference of Socialist Economists (CSE) Microprocessors Group, *Microelectronics: Capitalist Technology and the Working Class* (London: CSE Books, 1981).

8. Rachel Grossman, "Women's Place in the Integrated Circuit," *Southeast Asia Chronicle 66/Pacific Research* 9 (joint issue) (1979).

9. See R. E. Crum and C. Gudgin, *Non-Production Activities in U.K. Manufacturing Industry* (Brussels: Commission of European Communities, 1977).

10. J. Irvine, I. Miles, and J. Evans, eds., *Demystifying Social Statistics* (London: Pluto Press, 1979).

11. Ursula Huws, *Your Job in the Eighties* (London: Pluto Press, 1982).

12. See A. Game and C. Pringle, *Gender at Work* (London: Pluto Press, 1984); and C. Cockburn, *Brothers* (London: Pluto Press, 1983).

13. See Chapter 3 above.

14. R. Crompton and G. Jones, *White-Collar Proletariat* (Philadelphia: Temple Universtiy Press, 1984).

15. See Mike Cooley, *Architect or Bee?: The Human Technology Relationship* (Boston: South End Press, 1982); H. Wainwright and D. Elliot, *The Lucas Plan* (London: Alison and Busby, 1982).

16. Chapter 5 above.

17. See Committee for the Protection of Women in the Computer World (CPWCW), *Women and Microelectronics in Japan* (Tokyo: CPWCW, 1983).

18. Chapter 7 above; and U. Huws, J. Hurstfield, and R. Holmaat, *What Price Flexibility?*: *The Casualization of Women's Employment* (London: Low Pay Unit, 1989).

19. See M. Hepwort, *Geography of the Information Economy* (London: Bellhaven Press, 1989).

20. See Huws, Hurstfield, and Holmaat, *What Price Flexibility?*: *The Casualization of Women's Employment.*

21. See Ursula Huws, *VDU Hazards Handbook* (London: London Hazards Centre, 1987).

CHAPTER 9

1. Frances Cairncross, *The Death of Distance: How the Communications Revolution Will Change Our Lives* (Boston: Harvard Business School Press,1997); Diane Coyle, *Weightless World: Strategies for Managing the Digital Economy* (Oxford: Capstone Publishing,1997); Christopher Meyer and Stan Davis, *Blur: The Speed of Change in the Connected Economy* (South Port, Mass.: Addison-Wesley,1998); Don Tapscott, ed., *Blueprint for the Digital Economy: Wealth Creation in the Era of E-Business* (New York: McGraw Hill,1998); Don Tapscott, *The Digital Economy: Promise and Peril in the Age of Networked Intelligence* (New York: McGraw Hill, 1995); Dale Neef, ed., *The Economic Impact of Knowledge: Resources for the Knowledge-Based Economy* (Boston: Butterworth-Heinemann, 1998); Bob Norton and Cathy Smith, *Understanding the Virtual Organization,* (Hauppage, N.Y.: Barrons Educational, 1998).

2. In doing so, I have been helped immeasurably by discussions with the economist Henry Neuburger who has brought more skeptical rigor to these questions than anyone else I know. He is not responsible, of course, for any inadequacies in my arguments, for which I take full blame.

3. There is some encouraging evidence that this may have peaked, and that the old modernisms are beginning to reassert themselves. Nevertheless, we now have several generations of students already in or about to enter the intellectual labor market who have been taught to view the world through postmodernist lenses, and whose practices will be influenced by these views.

4. The critical realism of Roy Bhaskar seems to offer the most promising way forward currently on offer—see Roy Bhaskar, *A Realist Theory of Science* (London: Verso Books, 1997) and his *Dialectic: The Pulse of Freedom* (London: Verso Books, 1997). Also see Andrew Collier, *Critical Realism: An Introduction to Roy Bhaskar's Philosophy* (London: Verso Books, 1994); and the interesting discussion of Bhaskar's work in Meera Nanda, "Restoring the Real: Rethinking Social Constructivist Theories of Science," in *Socialist Register,* 1997, ed. Colin Leys and Leo Panitch (New York: Monthly Review Press, 1997).

5. Jean Baudrillard, *Simulacra and Simulation,* trans. Sheila Faria Glaser (Ann Arbor: University of Michigan Press, 1994).

6. Donna J. Haraway, *Simians, Cyborgs, and Women: The Reinvention of Nature* (London and New York: Routledge,1991).

7. His website is www. weightlesseconomy.com.

8. Danny T. Quah, "Increasingly Weightless Economies," *Bank of England Quarterly Bulletin,* February, 1997, p. 49.

9. Daniel Bell, *The Coming of Post-Industrial Society* (Basic Books, New York, 1973).

10. I did not have the resources while writing this article to demonstrate this conclusively on a national scale. However, in 1979-1980, with the invaluable help and guidance of Quentin Outram, I carried out a detailed study based on data from the decennial Censuses of Employment, supplemented in more recent years by data from Census of Employment, of service employment by occupation and industry (i.e., including those "service" workers whose employers were categorized in "manufacturing" or other non-service sectors) in one part of Britain, West Yorkshire. While doing this work-which focused particularly on women's employment—we were greatly struck by the almost exact parallel between the decline of domestic service and the expansion of other forms of service employment between 1901 and 1971. The report, which was published under the title *The Impact of New Technology on Women's Employment in West Yorkshire,* by Leeds Trade Union and Community Resource and Information Center, 1980, did not, unfortunately, draw attention to this finding.

11. C. H. Lee, *British Regional Employment Statistics,* 1841-1971 (Cambridge, England: Cambridge University Press, 1979).

12. Gøsta Esping-Andersen, *The Three Worlds of Welfare Capitalism* (Cambridge, England: Polity Press, 1990).

13. See Chapters 2 and 5 of this volume. The argument is summarized in Ursula Huws, "Consuming Fashions," *New Statesman* & *Society,* August 1988, and, most recently, in Ursula Huws, "What Is a Green-Red Economics?: The Future of Work" *ZMagazine,* September 1991.

14. Tim Jackson, *Material Concerns: Pollution, Profit and Quality of Life* (London: Routledge, 1996).

15. Department of the Environment, *Digest of Environmental Statistics,* information supplied by Friends of the Earth.

16. See David Noble, *Digital Diploma Mills* (New York: Monthly Review Press, 2002).

17. Diane Coyle, "Why Knowledge Is the New Engine of Economic Growth," *Independent,* 23 April 1998.

18. I am indebted to James Woudhuysen for this comparison.

19. Harry Braverman's *Labor and Monopoly Capital: The Degradation of Work in the Twentieth Century* (New York: Monthly Review Press, 1974).

20. "There Is No Finish Line—Running Shoes: The Follow-Up," *News from Irene,* no. 22 (March 1995), pp. 33-36.

21. The publication of Charles Babbage's *On the Economy of Machinery and Manufactures* in London in 1832 is as convenient a starting point as any to select for the systematic and conscious introduction of processes designed to reduce labor costs in manufacturing to a minimum.

22. Selected annually in a "Miss Pears" beauty contest that continued certainly up to the 1950s when I was a child, and quite possibly for many years afterward.

23. Sue Fernie and David Metcalf, "Hanging on the Telephone," *Centerpiece: The Magazine of Economic Performance* 3:1 (Spring 1998), p. 7; Research by Datamonitor, quoted in Una McLoughlin, "Call Center Staff Development," *T,* October 1997, pp. 18-21; *Incomes Data, Pay and Conditions in Call Center,* IDS Report 739, June 1997; G. Reardon, "Externalizing Information-Processing Work: Breaking the Logic of Spatial and Work Organization," UN University Institute for New Technologies Conference on Globalized Information Society: Employment Implications, Maastricht, 17-19 October 1996.

24. Martin Shaw and Ian Miles, "The Social Roots of Statistical Knowledge" in *Demystifying Social Statistics,* ed. John Irvine, Ian Miles, and Jeff Evans (London: Pluto Press,1981), p. 30.

25. Danny Quah, "Policies for the Weightless Economy," lecture to the Social Market Foundation, London, 21 April 1998.

26. Luc Soete distinguishes three forms in which knowledge becomes embedded in a commodity (or, in his language "contributes to growth"). These are "easily transferable codifiable knowledge," "non-codifiable knowledge, also known as tacit knowledge (skills)," and "codified knowledge." See Luc Soete, "The Challenges of Innovation" in *IPTS Report* 7, Institute for Prospective Technological Studies, Seville, September 1996, pp. 7-13. This typology is extremely useful for analyzing the components of value added but less so for keeping the labor process in focus.

27. This is certainly the practice in the West London district of Southall, which houses a large population from the Indian subcontinent and one of whose major industries is the preparation of curries and other Indian foods for British supermarket chains. See Ursula Huws, *Changes in the West London Economy* (London: West London Training and Enterprise Council, 1992).

28. The excellent bimonthly *GenEthics News: Genetic Engineering, Ethics and the Environment,* chronicles new instances of this in every issue.

29. This is documented in the National Union of Journalists' monthly magazine, *The Journalist.*

30. Danny Quah, "As Productive as a French Farmer," *Asian Wall Street Journal,* 29 September 1997.

31. Henry Neuburger, "Thoughts on the Productivity Paradox," unpublished

paper, n.d., p. 1. Arguing that measurement of total factor productivity is circular, he selected labor productivity as providing a more robust indicator.

32. Ibid, p. 9.

33. Jeff Madrick, "Computers: Waiting for the Revolution," *The New York Review of Books*, 26 March 1998.

34. Sue Himmelweit, discussion of ONS Households satellite accounts, Royal Statistical Society, November 1997, quoted in Neuburger, "Thoughts on the Productivity Paradox."

35. Julie Askalen, Olav Bjerkholt, Charlotte Koren, and Stig-Olof Olsson, "Care Work in Household and Market: Productivity, Economic Growth and Welfare," paper submitted to the IAFFE-sponsored session at the ASSA meeting, Chicago, 3-5 January 1998. I am indebted to Sue Himmelweit for bringing this important research to my attention. Henry Neuburger has partially tested this hypothesis in the United Kingdom by modeling—in the form of household satellite accounts—two areas of activity, child care and catering, using both input and output measures. He concluded that "conventional GDP by omitting unpaid child care understated growth in the 1960s and overstated it in the 1970s." See Henry Neuburger, "Modifying GDP," unpublished paper, n.d., p. 2. For an interesting discussion of the development of satellite accounts and social accounting matrices, see Neuburger, "Measuring Economic Activity," unpublished paper, n.d. The evidence is clearly complex and contradictory, but such studies point up the incomplete picture gained from the conventional accounting procedures.

36. I have discussed this literature at some length in Ursula Huws, *Teleworking: An Overview of the Research,* joint publication of the Department of Transport, Department of Trade and Industry, Department of the Environment, Department for Education and Employment, and Employment Service, London, July 1996; and Ursula Huws, "Beyond Anecdotes: On Quantifying the Globalization of Information-Processing Work." United Nations University Institute for New Technologies Conference on *Globalized Information Society: Employment Implications,* Maastricht, 17-19 October 1996.

37. Paul Hirst and Grahame Thompson, *Globalization in Question* (Oxford, England: Polity Press, 1996), p. 27.

38. I have discussed this problem in "Beyond Anecdotes: On Quantifying the Globalization of Information Processing Work."

39. Luc Soete and Karin Kamp, *The "BIT TAX": The Case for Further Research,* MERIT, University of Maastricht, 12 August 1996.

40. Richard I. Cook, M.D., Cognitive Technologies Lab., Dept. of Anesthesia and Critical Care, University of Chicago, quoted in *Risks-Forum Digest* 19.75, forwarded by Red Rock Eater News Service (pagre@weber.ucsd.edu), May 1998.

41. Mike Holderness, "The Internet: Enabling Whom?, When? and Where?," *The Information Revolution and Economic and Social Exclusion in the Developing Countries,* UNU/INTECH Workshop, Maastricht, 23-25 October 1996.

42. I have summarized these, and other related factors, in a number of publications including, Ursula Huws, *Follow-Up to the White Paper—Teleworking,* European Commission Directorate General V, September 1994, also published in *Social Europe, Supplement 3,* European Commission DGV, 1995; Huws, *Teleworking: An Overview of the Research;* and Chapter 7 above.

43. Ursula Huws, Sheila Honey, and Stephen Morris, *Teleworking and Rural Development* (Swindon, England: Rural Development Commission, 1996).

CHAPTER 10

1. *Analytica,* e-mail newsletter, March 2000.

2. E-mail from Alice de Wolff to Ursula Huws, April 2000.

3. R. Crompton and G. Jones, *White-Collar Proletariat: De-Skilling and Gender in Clerical Work* (London and Basingstoke: Macmillan, 1984); E. O. Wright, "The Class Structure of Advanced Capitalist Societies" in *Class, Crisis and the State* (London: Verso, 1979); N. Poulantzas, *Classes in Contemporary Capitalism* (London: New Left Books, 1975); E. O. Wright, "The Class Structure of Advanced Capitalist Societies" in his *Class, Crisis and the State (London: Verso, 1979).*

4. K. Marx, *Capital,* vol. 3 (London: Lawrence and Wishart, 1974), pp. 299-300, cited in Crompton and Jones, *White-Collar Proletariat,* p. 8.

5. G. Marshall, H. Newby, D. Rose, and C. Vogler, *Social Class in Modern Britain (London: Hutchinson, 1988),* p. 23.

6. C. Wright Mills, *White Collar: The American Middle Classes* (New York: Oxford University Press, 1951); D. Lockwood, *The Black-Coated Worker* (London: George Allen and Unwin, 1958).

7. Quoted in H. Braverman, *Labor and Monopoly Capital: The Degradation of Work in the Twentieth Century* (New York: Monthly Review Press, 1974), p. 296.

8. Mills, *White Collar,* pp. 352-353.

9. Marshall et al., p. 68.

10. R. Sennett and J. Cobb, *The Hidden Injuries of Class* (New York: W. W. Norton, 1972).

11. Braverman, *Labor and Monopoly Capital.*

12. J. H. Goldthorpe, *Social Mobility and Class Structure in Modern Britain* (Oxford, England: Clarendon Press, 1980) and "On the Service Class: Its Formation and Future," in *Social Class and the Division of Labor,* ed. Giddens and Mackenzie (Cambridge: Cambridge University Press, 1982).

13. I have discussed some of these ideas at greater length in Chapter 8 above.

14. J. Tepperman, *Not Servants, Not Machines: Office Workers Speak Out* (Boston: Beacon Press, 1976); J. Gregory, *Race Against Time* (Cleveland: 9 to 5, 1981); Marianne Craig, *The Office Worker's Survival Handbook* (London: BSSRS, 1981); Crompton and Jones, *White-Collar Proletariat;* A. Game and R. Pringle, *Gender at Work* (London: Pluto Press, 1984); L. K. Howe, *Pink Collar: Inside the World of Women's Work* (New York: Avon, 1977); R. Howard, *Brave New Workplace* (New York: Viking/Penguin, 1985); L. Siegel and J. Markoff, *The High Cost of High Tech,* (New York: Harper and Row, 1985).

15. These are discussed in U. Huws, N. Jagger, and S. O'Regan, *Teleworking and Globalization* (Brighton: Institute for Employment Studies, 1999) and include A. Posthuma, *The Internationalization of Clerical Work: A Study of Offshore Office Services in the Caribbean,* SPRU Occasional Paper no. 24 (University of Sussex, Brighton: 1987); Antonio Soares, "The Hard Life of the Unskilled Workers in New Technologies: Data Entry Clerks in Brazil" in *Human Aspects in Computing,* ed. H. J. Bullinger (Amsterdam: Elsevier Science Publishers, 1991) and "Telework and Communication in Data Processing Centers in Brazil" in *Technology-Mediated Communication,* ed. U. E. Gattiker (Berlin and New York: Walter de Gruyter, 1992); D. Pantin, *Export-Based Information Processing in the Caribbean, with Particular Respect to Offshore Data Processing,* (Geneva: FIET, 1995); R. Pearson, "Gender and New Technology in the Caribbean: New Work for Women?," in *Gender Analysis in Development,* ed. J. Momsen, Discussion Paper no. 5 (University of East Anglia, Norwich: 1991); and R. Pearson and S. Mitter, "Employment and Working Conditions of Low-Skilled Information-Processing Workers in Less Developed Countries," *International Labor Review,* April 1993.

16. Exceptions to this are C. May's analysis in *The Rise of Web-Back Labor: Global Information Society and the International Division of Labor* (Plymouth: Plymouth International Studies Center, University of Plymouth, 1999) and the pioneering field studies of Jan Sinclair Jones, in various unpublished papers and in "First You See It, Now You Don't: Home-Based Telework in the Global Context," Working Paper presented to the Australian Sociology Association Conference, Monash University, Melbourne, 5-7 December 1999.

17. Braverman, *Labor and Monopoly Capital,* p. 303.

18. K. Marx, *Capital,* vol. 3 (London: Lawrence and Wishart, 1974), pp. 299-300, quoted in Crompton and Jones, *White-Collar Proletariat,* p. 9.

19. See chapter 9.

20. See chapter 5.

21. Strategic alliances are discussed, *inter alia,* by J. H. Dunning in *The Globalization of Business* (London: Routledge, 1993).

22. F. Parkin, *Marxism and Class Theory* (London: Tavistock, 1979).

23. E. Wolff and W. Baumol, in *The Information Economy: The Implications of Unbalanced Growth,* ed. L. Osberg et al. (Quebec: Institute for Research on Public Policy, 1989); M. Lavoie and P. Therrien, *Employment Effects of Computerization* (Ottawa: Human Resources Development Canada Applied Research Branch, 1999).

24. European Labor Force Survey data, Eurostat.

25. M. Campbell and M. Daley, "Self-Employment: Into the 1990s," *Employment Gazette,* June 1992.

26. N. Meager and.1. Moralee, "Self-Employment and the Distribution of Income," in *New Inequalities,* ed. J. Hill (Cambridge: Cambridge University Press, 1996).

27. Ibid.

28. A. Rajan and P. van Eupen, *Tomorrow's People* (Kent, England: CREATE, 1998).

29. See chapter 3.

30. Quoted in Barbara Ehrenreich and Deirdre English, *For Her Own Good* (London: Pluto Press, 1979).

31. See B. Young, "The 'Mistress' and the 'Maid' in the Globalized Economy," *Socialist Register,* 2001.

32. E-mail from G. Greenfield, Globalization Monitor, Hong Kong, June 2000.

33. Quoted in Theo Nichols, "Social Class: Official, Sociological and Marxist," in *Demystifying Social Statistics,* ed. J. Irvine, I. Miles, and J. Evans (London: Pluto Press, 1979), p.159.

34. Crompton and Jones, *White-Collar Proletariat,* p. 27. 35 Eurostat data, 1999.

36. UNCTAD and PIKOM data, quoted in S. Mitter and U. Efendioglu, "Relocation of Information-Processing Work: Implications for Trade Between Asia and the European Union," unpublished paper (Maastricht: UN University Institute of Technology, 1997).

37. S. Khilnani, *The Idea of India* (Delhi: Penguin, 1998), p. 148.

38 E-mail from S. Gothoskhar to U. Huws, June 2000.

39. Jones, "First You See It, Now You Don't: Home-Based Telework in the Global Context."

40. This point is made by P. Lloyd in his *A Third World Proletariat* (London: George Allen and Unwin, 1982).

41. R. Pearson, "Gender and New Technology in the Caribbean: New Work for Women?" in *Gender Analysis in Development,* ed. Momsen; Soares, "The Hard Life of the Unskilled Workers in New Technologies: Data Entry Clerks in Brazil."

42. Jones, "First You See It, Now You Don't."

INDEX